W9-AQT-737

George Gissing

Twayne's English Authors Series

Herbert Sussman, Editor

Northeastern University

TEAS 346

GEORGE GISSING
(1857–1903)
Photograph by G. & J. Hall

George Gissing

By Robert L. Selig

Purdue University Calumet

Twayne Publishers • Boston

George Gissing

Robert L. Selig

Published by Twayne Publishers
A Division of G. K. Hall & Company
70 Lincoln Street
Boston, Massachusetts 02111

Book Production by John Amburg
Book Design by Barbara Anderson

Printed on permanent/durable acid-free paper and bound in The United States of America.

Library of Congress Cataloging in Publication Data

Selig, Robert L.
George Gissing.

(Twayne's English authors series ; TEAS 346)
Bibliography: p. 161
Includes index.
1. Gissing, George Robert, 1857–1903
—Criticism and interpretation.
I. Title. II. Series.
PR4717.S4 1983 823'.8 82–15494
ISBN 0–8057–6831–9

Contents

About the Author

Robert L. Selig is Professor of English at Purdue University Calumet, with a specialty in nineteenth-century and early twentieth-century British literature and particularly in the novel. His publications include *Elizabeth Gaskell: A Reference Guide* (Boston: G. K. Hall, 1977) and articles on George Gissing in *Nineteenth-Century Fiction*, *Studies in English Literature*, and the *Gissing Newsletter*. In collaboration with Professor Pierre Coustillas, Dr. Selig has published further Gissing articles in the *Times Literary Supplement* (London), the *Book Collector*, and the *Gissing Newsletter*. He participated in a Special Session on "Gissing and Women" at the 1978 National Convention of the Modern Language Association of America. He has also published articles on E. M. Forster, George Eliot, and Henry James in the *Journal of Modern Literature* and *Nineteenth-Century Fiction*. In addition, Dr. Selig's own short stories have appeared in *Accent* and *Ascent*.

Dr. Selig received the Bachelor of Arts in English (1954) from the University of North Carolina at Chapel Hill, the Master's (1958) and Doctor's (1965) degrees in English from Columbia University. From 1956 to 1957 he served as a National Woodrow Wilson Fellow at Columbia University. From 1961 to 1967, Dr. Selig taught at Queens College of the City University of New York.

Preface

On 13 June 1888 Gissing felt so dissatisfied with four manuscript pages of his novel *The Nether World* (1889) that he spent the whole day rewriting them. Weary and disgruntled, he later set down in his diary a blunt self-criticism of a persistent tendency in his fiction up till then: "it is poor stuff, all this idealism; I'll never go in for it again" [*London and the Life of Literature in Late Victorian England: The Diary of George Gissing, Novelist*, ed. Pierre Coustillas (Lewisburg, Pa., 1978), p. 32]. Although literary historians have generally classified Gissing's entire output under "realism," his early writings combine detailed representations of social actualities with idealized portraits of heroes and heroines nobler and more sensitive than the world that surrounds them or, in fact, that surrounds the reader. In Gissing's first six novels, he remains strongly influenced by a sentimental-idealist tradition that, for more than three centuries, had often diluted supposedly "realistic" novels with elements of romance. He wrote his finest works after his 13 June farewell to literary "idealism." Such Gissing books as *New Grub Street* (1891) and *Born in Exile* (1892) stand as major achievements in the history of English "realism"—a "realism" that increasingly discarded the old "idealizing" conventions.

Because "realism," like "idealism," works both as literary convention and as imaginative response to social actualities, this study places Gissing's creative achievement within an accompanying cultural and historical perspective. Gissing's books themselves demand not only a knowledge of other comparable books, but also of many nonbookish matters: conditions of working-class life in the late-nineteenth century, qualifications for becoming one of the gentry, changes in private morality caused by declining religious faith, challenges by late-Victorian feminists to inequities between the sexes, and various repercussions upon writers and their readers of expanding mass communication. To understand Gissing's place in English letters, one must also understand the culture in which he lived and upon which he focused his books.

This study examines all of Gissing's twenty-two novels and his four books of nonfiction. It also surveys his unjustly neglected and numerous short stories. The work proceeds in broadly chronological fashion, but it groups similar books together in individual chapters. Chapter 1 reviews Gissing's troubled life. The rest of the study explores Gissing's writings in the following order: working-class novels, early middle-class ones, the remarkable *New Grub Street* and *Born in Exile*, three novels dealing with marriage problems, four novelettes, five late novels, two and a half decades of short stories, and the nonfiction. Although Gissing's *New Grub Street* remains today his most famous work, he was anything but a one-book man.

Robert L. Selig

Purdue University Calumet

Acknowledgments

I am indebted to the Henry W. and Albert A. Berg Collection of the New York Public Library, Astor, Lenox, and Tilden Foundations, for having allowed me access to various unpublished letters.

I am indebted to the Beinecke Rare Book and Manuscript Library of Yale University for having allowed me access to various unpublished documents and letters.

I wish to thank Purdue University Calumet for granting me a half-sabbatical leave to work on the Gissing book.

I should also like to thank Professor Jacob Korg for encouraging me to undertake this project in the first place.

Finally, I should like to express my indebtedness to Professor Pierre Coustillas, who provided me with a print of the frontispiece photograph, read my first chapter, and informed me of his newest findings about George Gissing's life.

List of Abbreviations

CD	George Gissing, *Charles Dickens: A Critical Study* (St. Clair Shores, Mich., 1976)
CS	George Gissing, *Critical Studies of the Works of Charles Dickens* (New York, 1965)
EF	George Gissing, *Essays & Fiction* (Baltimore, 1970)
GN	The *Gissing Newsletter*
Goode, *GG*	John Goode, *George Gissing: Ideology and Fiction* (New York, 1979)
HC	George Gissing, *The House of Cobwebs* (London, 1931)
HOE	George Gissing, *Human Odds and Ends: Stories and Sketches* (London, 1898)
Korg, *GG*	Jacob Korg, *George Gissing: A Critical Biography* (Seattle, 1963)
SS	George Gissing, *Stories and Sketches* (London, 1938)
VC	George Gissing, *A Victim of Circumstances and Other Stories* (Boston, 1927)

Chronology

1857 George Robert Gissing born at Wakefield, Yorkshire, 22 November.

1870 Father, Thomas Waller Gissing, died suddenly, 28 December.

1871 Accompanied by two brothers, entered Lindow Grove, a Quaker boarding school at Alderley Edge, Cheshire.

1872 Won highest rank within Manchester district in Oxford Local Examination, entitling him to three years' free tuition at Owens College, Manchester. Entered Owens in October but continued to live at Lindow Grove School.

1874 Matriculated with high honors at University of London—then merely a degree-examining institution for such colleges as Owens.

1875 Moved to private lodgings in Manchester. Won exhibitions in English and Latin and also won a Shakespeare scholarship.

1876 Extending Easter seaside vacation with the prostitute Marianne Helen (Nell) Harrison, cut April classes at Owens. On 31 May arrested for thefts in college cloakroom; on 6 June convicted and sentenced to a month at hard labor; on 7 June expelled from Owens. Sailed for United States to start new life. Published art review in *Commonwealth* (Boston).

1877 Taught briefly at Waltham, Massachusetts, public high school. Traveled to Chicago and published first fiction, "The Sins of the Fathers," in *Chicago Tribune* of 10

March. Published at least nineteen other short stories in Chicago newspapers from March through July. Returned to eastern United States and published story in New York City monthly. Sailed for England in September and arrived 3 October.

1879 Long after resuming life with Nell Harrison, he married her on 27 October. Earned money as tutor and clerk.

1880 Brother, William, died of consumption, 16 April. *Workers in the Dawn* published at author's own expense. Gained friendship of Frederic Harrison.

1882 The novel "Mrs. Grundy's Enemies" accepted but never published.

1883 Separated from Nell Harrison.

1884 *The Unclassed.* "Phoebe."

1886 *Isabel Clarendon* and *Demos.* Trafalgar Square Riot occurred 8 February.

1887 *Thyrza.*

1888 Nell Harrison died 29 February. *A Life's Morning.* Began five month trip abroad, mainly in Italy.

1889 Completed Italian trip. *The Nether World.* Began trip to Greece and Italy.

1890 Illness in Naples diagnosed as lung congestion. Completed Greek and Italian trip. *The Emancipated.* Met Edith Underwood.

1891 *New Grub Street.* "Letty Coe." Married Edith Underwood 25 February. Son, Walter, born 10 December.

1892 *Denzil Quarrier* and *Born in Exile.*

1893 *The Odd Women.* "A Victim of Circumstances," "Lou and Liz," "The Day of Silence."

1894 *In the Year of Jubilee.* "Comrades in Arms."

1895 *Eve's Ransom*, *Sleeping Fires*, and *The Paying Guest.* "A

Lodger in Maze Pond," "The Poet's Portmanteau," and "An Old Maid's Triumph."

1896 Second son, Alfred, born 20 January. "The Foolish Virgin" and "The Schoolmaster's Vision."

1897 *The Whirlpool.* Ill from lung congestion again, he left wife. Departed for six-month Italian trip that later provided material for *By the Ionian Sea.*

1898 Completed Italian trip. *Charles Dickens: A Critical Study*, *Human Odds and Ends*, and *The Town Traveller.* "One Way of Happiness." Met Gabrielle Marie Edith Fleury on 6 July. Saw wife for last time on 7 September.

1899 *The Crown of Life.* Preface to *The Pickwick Papers.* Unable to obtain divorce, began to live as "man and wife" with Gabrielle Fleury in France, following a 7 May "marriage" ceremony.

1900 *By the Ionian Sea* serialized. "The House of Cobwebs." Prefaces to *Nicholas Nickleby*, *Bleak House*, and *Oliver Twist.*

1901 *Our Friend the Charlatan.* Book publication of *By the Ionian Sea.* "A Daughter of the Lodge." Prefaces to *The Old Curiosity Shop* and *Barnaby Rudge.* Went to Arcachon for healthy climate. Condition diagnosed as emphysema.

1902 Serialization begun of "An Author at Grass," later called *The Private Papers of Henry Ryecroft.* "Christopherson." Edith Underwood Gissing committed to insane asylum. With Gabrielle Fleury and her mother, he moved to Saint-Jean-de-Luz for healthy climate.

1903 Book publication of *The Private Papers of Henry Ryecroft.* Moved to Ispoure (Saint-Jean-Pied-de-Port) and died there, 28 December.

1904 *Veranilda* published posthumously.

1905 *Will Warburton* published posthumously.

Chapter One

A Life of Errors and Revisions

Early Years

A central impulse in Gissing's life—his love of books and studiousness—came from his father's class-conscious example. Although Thomas Waller Gissing (1829–1870) made his living as a pharmacist in the mill town of Wakefield, this son of a Suffolk shoemaker had an autodidact's reverence for literature and also for elegance of speech. Indeed, Gissing's father actually published three books of verse and two books on botany—literary accomplishments of which George remained proud well into his own career.[1] In a late essay on Dickens, George explicitly associates the death of his own father, the amateur Gissing writer, with the death of this great Victorian novelist, both having occurred in 1870:

> Time went by, and one day I stood before a picture newly hung in the children's room. It was a large wood-cut, published (I think) by *The Illustrated London News*, and called "The Empty Chair." Then for the first time I heard of Dickens's home and knew that he had lived at that same Gadshill of which Shakespeare spoke. Not without awe did I see the picture of the room which now was tenantless; I remember, too, a curiosity which led me to look closely at the writing-table and the objects upon it, at the comfortable, round-backed chair, at the book-shelves behind; I began to ask myself how books were written, and how the men lived who wrote them. It is my last glimpse

of childhood. Six months later there was an empty chair in my own home, and the tenor of my life was broken.[2]

The passage salutes George's father as an author, like Dickens, with his own writer's chair. The sentences about the two empty chairs link Thomas Waller Gissing, Dickens, and even Shakespeare in the great republic of letters, which George himself had joined by the time that he wrote this elegiac but proud paragraph.

George's reminiscences of childhood tend to counterpoise his father's love of books with his mother's love of the Church—a piety that father and son united in deploring. On Sunday mornings, his father taught George to recite Tennyson, but mother herded her children to Anglican services. Margaret Bedford Gissing (1832–1913), the daughter of a respectable Droitwich solicitor, remained so faithful to Low Church observances that George wondered why his father could never persuade his wife to alter her convictions.[3] Clearly enough, she exercised a strong maternal influence on George's two younger sisters—an influence at cross current to Thomas Gissing's teachings. The son recalled how his father made fun of his young daughter Madge for observing Sabbath rules.[4] Yet if Mrs. Gissing's daughters, Madge and Ellen, remained pious churchgoers all of their lives,[5] George derived from his father a Matthew Arnold-like faith that literature could fill the void left by a disappearing religion.

The novelist's enduring respect for his father as a self-made man of letters seems all the more striking in view of George's contempt for Thomas Gissing's working-class relatives. The son admired the father for what he had escaped from as much as for what he had achieved. George's memories of Thomas Waller Gissing resemble the many portraits in Gissing's early novels of working-class characters whose love of books and art sets them miles above the culture of their proletarian friends and relatives. Some years after Thomas Gissing's premature death, George snubbed his father's own father out of sheer class disdain. Robert Foulsham Gissing, the grandfather, had written twice to his grandson to complain that George had shunned him as a mere low relation. To brother Algernon, George admitted privately that he felt distaste for grandfather and for grandfather's whole family, even though they lived nearby. George grumbled that the working-class Gissing lacked respect for art and for intellectual effort.[6] In this priggish reaction to an old man's hurt feelings, the youthful author revealed his basic contempt for a shoemaker grandfather who could not comprehend the writer's way of life—a life pursued in turn by Thomas Waller Gissing and by George Gissing himself.

When Thomas Gissing died, thirteen-year-old George had already committed himself to the ardent study of literature. At Harrison's Back Lane School, he had begun Latin at eight, Greek at age ten, and had taken to them both with unusual skill and pleasure. Eventually, he even made boyish fun of his self-taught father's mistaken idea that classical poetry rhymed. Yet the sudden death of the parent who had encouraged George's early efforts to be brilliant left him with a permanent sense of loss. Some of Thomas Gissing's Wakefield friends tried to fill the void by getting George admitted immediately, along with his two younger brothers, to a Quaker boarding school for boys at Alderley Edge, some thirteen miles south of Manchester. And, in fact, George clearly welcomed the authority of his male teachers at the Lindow Grove School as a comforting substitute for the lost father. Many years later, Gissing recalled his undimmed affection for them and, above all, for the headmaster, Mr. James Wood, who, like Gissing's father, read to the boys from works of high literary seriousness—perhaps "something from Dr. Arnold; a passage well chosen and impressively delivered." George repaid his teachers at Alderley Edge by prodigious efforts of study, which in 1872 won him the highest rank within the Manchester district in the Oxford Local Examination.[7]

Gissing's excellence in the Local Examination earned him a three-year scholarship to Owens College, Manchester, but with an oddly significant twist; this fifteen-year-old prize winner attended college without leaving secondary school. He continued to live in a Lindow Grove dormitory and rode the train to his Manchester classes. Still secure in the haven that had sheltered him since

Thomas Gissing's death, still accompanied by two younger brothers at Lindow Grove, still surrounded by his former schoolmasters, George excelled at college. One session he earned so many books as prizes that he had to carry them home in a cab. He won an English poetry prize and a Shakespeare scholarship. Because the college itself could not grant degrees, he matriculated with high honors under the auspices of the University of London, then a mere degree-examining institution. Through the University of London, he also passed his intermediate Bachelor's examination in the First Division, and he won highest honors along with exhibitions (scholarships) in both English and Latin. At just under eighteen, he seemed on the way to a brilliant career as professor of literature and the classics. Then, with only one more set of examinations needed for the Bachelor's degree, Gissing kicked away his academic future by reckless and foolish misbehavior.[8]

Disgrace and Exile

The crisis came in the academic year 1875–76. George's mother decided that he was now old enough to live in college surroundings. Unfortunately for the boy, Owens College itself had no dormitories yet, so that George had to live alone in a Manchester rooming house, off in a squalid byway. Before this drastic change, he had labored at his studies ascetically, often from 4:00 A.M. to 12:00 P.M.[9] Yet after no more than half a year alone in a harsh urban setting, the scholarly ascetic entangled himself with a Manchester prostitute even younger than himself. By early April he was cutting all his classes in order to prolong a seaside vacation at Southport with her.[10]

In his affair with seventeen-year-old Nell Harrison, Gissing tried to impose upon a brutal reality the form of sentimental fiction. Prostitutes worked the bars that surrounded Cobden house, the temporary home of the college in Gissing's first year, and, although Owens had moved to a better location by the time of George's involvement with Nell, the legend remained of the Owens College porter who had been "inveigled" by a prostitute into an adjacent bar, "robbed," and "ejected" stark naked.[11] Indeed, Nell's rooms at Water Street stood only a few blocks away from the sinkhole of the college's original neighborhood. Yet after Gissing's sexual initiation by her in these unromantic circumstances, he insisted that he had "fallen in love." He continued to insist upon his high-minded affection even as the affair grew more sordid. Although he told his best friend at college, John George Black, of his undying love for the prostitute, a weeping and tipsy Nell promptly seduced Black and then asked him to "say nothing to" Gissing. When Black revealed the truth to him, Gissing felt more betrayed by his friend than by the girl. Yet the schoolmates became reconciled by a common misfortune: they had both contracted venereal disease from Nell. But instead of taking warning from this sexual fiasco, Gissing tried to reform Nell by providing her with money to keep off the streets and a sewing machine to make an honest living. In order to get the money for her, George stole cash, books, and even coats from the Owens College Cloakroom. On 31 May 1876 he was caught in the act of theft by a hidden plainclothesman. On 6 June Gissing was convicted and sentenced to a month at hard labor in prison. While he served his term, Owens College expelled him. And one day after Gissing's release, Owens stripped him of his Shakespeare scholarship.[12] With an almost unbearable irony, the disgraced young man lost his chance for any further work in an English university in the very month when he might have been taking the final Bachelor's examinations.

Young George seems to have viewed his catastrophic actions through a haze of bookish sentimentality. Either at Manchester or later, he gave Nell a copy of his father's "Margaret," a poetic defense of fallen women, as a literary inducement to reform. The fifty-four Spenserian stanzas of the poem tell a neo-Wordsworthian story of a warm-hearted maiden seduced by her lover, made pregnant, abandoned, and yet still pure of soul:

> Yet on her open soul is virtue set;
> And spite of prudish sneers and ribaldry,
> A purer heart and fairer form ne'er met.

'Twas love that bade her maiden honour flee,
And love still keeps her pure as virgin purity![13]

Gissing's father appended to his poem more than four pages of passionate feminist prose, including one sentence that applied to Nell like a custom-made personal footnote:

> These people are surprised that these individuals never reform; forgetting that if they once made a step towards reformation, they—the vituperators—would be the first to spurn them back to their old life, through refusing to trust in their sincerity.[14]

In 1888, when reform had failed and Gissing found Nell dead at thirty in a grim London rooming house, he noted in his diary, as the climax of his anguish, "a copy of my Father's 'Margaret' which she had preserved" even in her final degradation.[15]

Even after his disgrace and imprisonment, Gissing still saw his relationship with Nell through the spectacles of sentimental literature. Either on his own or through the help of friends, George shipped himself off to the United States in order to escape his scandalous past, but he insisted upon viewing this perfectly sensible step as a means to an ultimate reunion with Nell in America. In a clearly personal poem written shortly before he sailed, Gissing revealed his happy-ending hope of making good in the United States and bringing Nell to live with him there. His undistinguished verses seek to comfort a tearful woman who will remain behind while the speaker crosses the ocean in search of a fresh start.[16]

A few weeks later, his first letters home from Boston show his resolve to become a professional writer as a way to provide a New World home for Nell. Through a female doctor in Boston named Zakrzewska, who held literary salons, Gissing met William Lloyd Garrison, the elderly writer and abolitionist. George quickly boasted to his brother that Garrison is "my principal friend here. . . . He knows the editor of the *Atlantic Monthly* . . . very well, and thinks he can perhaps get me a place on its staff. . . ." George also told of a critical essay that he would submit to the *Atlantic.* Although nothing came of the possible staff job or even of the essay, Gissing quickly broke into print with an art review in the *Commonwealth* (Boston).[17] Encouraged by this small success, he continued to write but apparently could not sell more work. As so often later in his life, he had to turn from literature to the stopgap of teaching. The reunion promised in his poetic farewell to Nell might take somewhat longer than planned.

He found an assistant teachership in French, German, and English at a public high school in Waltham, Massachusetts. But almost certainly, this academic perch seemed highly precarious. To an American unfamiliar with the British system of multiple examinations for the Bachelor's degree, Gissing's university certificates might even have suggested that he had actually finished the B.A. If, in fact, he won his job through misunderstood credentials, he must have felt unnerved when a newspaper reporter in Waltham asked him "where I came from and where I had studied."[18] A few years later in a similar situation, when Gissing was tutoring Frederic Harrison's sons, a former Owens classmate unmasked the hapless tutor as a convict expelled in disgrace, and only Harrison's humanity saved George from dismissal. In any case, by the end of February, probably before the high school could have checked his credentials in England, Gissing abruptly left his teaching job.[19]

With Nell still very much on his mind, Gissing resumed his campaign to become a professional writer. Apparently seeking literary material about his adopted country, he traveled west to Chicago, where the editor of the *Tribune* accepted the young man's audacious offer to write short stories for the paper. Yet his first published story, in the *Chicago Tribune* of 10 March 1877, deals only partly with America. The heroine and hero resemble Nell and George—she a streetwalker from an English industrial city and he a departed lover toiling to succeed for her by teaching school in New England—although both meet death through a tangle of melodramatic crises. In about four months in Chicago, Gissing published at least twenty short stories, whose basic immaturity matters less than their evidence of literary stamina, the sheer will to go on writing. Yet because he earned only eighteen dollars for each, by July in Chicago he found himself almost starving.[20] Leaving that city, he wandered eastward again, in search of receptive editors, but soon ran out of money: he had to live on peanuts in Troy, New York; he got a story published in New York's *Appletons' Journal* for forty-five dollars; and he survived for weeks in New England as an assistant to an itinerant photographer. By summer's end Gissing had had enough of literary struggles in America. In September he set sail for Liverpool; for renewed efforts at writing on home territory; and, most importantly, for Nell.[21]

Marital Disaster, Release, and Frustration

He arrived in England on 3 October 1877 and apparently soon went to Nell to resume their old relationship, this time in London—the literary captial.[22] Yet even as they renewed their sexual past, Gissing avoided his Owens College mistake of allowing his infatuation to divert him from his bookish career. He immediately plunged into a full-length novel and worked as hard at writing as he had once worked at his college literary studies, which, in fact, he now continued on his own. And he avoided his Chicago error of relying for support on writing alone: he began to tutor stray pupils and even took a temporary clerkship. In addition, on his twenty-first birthday he received some £300 from a trust fund left by his father, and Gissing tried to save this new capital by such thrift as living on lentils and continuing to teach for a mere trickle of shillings.[23] When he finished his novel but could not get it published, he sensibly resolved that "the next must be better" and started it immediately. Yet he also kept on earning small sums through the odds and ends of teaching and clerking.[24]

Nevertheless, all of Gissing's prudent efforts to revise his past mistakes as Nell's would-be redeemer foundered on her alcoholism: she stubbornly defied redemption. She drank constantly, using up their cash; she brawled in public places; and sometimes she even, apparently, returned to prostitution to gain more liquor money.[25] In the second half of *Workers in the Dawn* (1880), his first surviving novel, Gissing describes the hero's appalling mismarriage with an alcoholic prostitute, Carrie Mitchell, obviously drawn from Nell. Yet, extraordinarily enough, as he finished the final pages, he actually married Carrie's real-life counterpart, with whom he had lived for two whole years of unblissful nonweddedness.[26] He probably hoped that marriage formalized in a church would encourage sober faithfulness by enhancing Nell's self-dignity. But, if anything, she grew worse after the wedding: she cheated him of money for drink, fell down drunk in the street, hid a gin bottle among her belongings, had to be sent away for a rest cure, got herself arrested for disturbing the peace, and needed a paid companion to restrain her from drinking and brawling. Yet he endured her drunken capers, her frequent disappearances, and kept taking her back until 1883, when he finally admitted the hopelessness of ever reforming Nell. They separated for good, but he went on supporting her.[27] One can speculate why he endured her carryings on for so long. In addition to the jumble of his emotions about this woman—physical attachment, love, pity, guilt—Gissing undoubtedly felt that, in giving up on Nell, he reduced his disgrace at Owens to a mere senseless act, a sacrifice for absolutely nothing.

Yet something constructive emerged from his troubled years with Nell. Although she served as both a motive and hindrance, her problems spurred Gissing to hard work at novel writing. *Workers in the Dawn* (1880) went begging for a publisher, but at last Gissing used a chunk of his father's trust fund to pay for vanity publication. If such a tactic usually leads to the valley of the shadow of oblivion, Gissing's desperate gamble won him, in fact, important literary friends. He sent a copy of *Workers* to Frederic Harrison, a leader of the English Positivist Society, and declared in a covering letter that the book owed much to Harrison's Comtist teachings about a secular religion of humanity to replace supernatural worship. Harrison liked the novel and its writer well enough to introduce him to a literary circle including John Morley, editor of both the *Fortnightly* and the *Pall Mall Gazette.* Morley, in his turn, talked the young man up, even to

Matthew Arnold, and found Gissing journalistic assignments. To help him support himself, Harrison offered his own sons for Gissing to tutor at rather good pay and also found him other pupils from well-to-do acquaintances. And without the help of his patron, the struggling young writer made two close literary friendships that remained important to him long after his years with Nell: the German exile Eduard Bertz, who, as translator and editor, would help promote Gissing's works in Germany; and a free-lance writer named Morley Roberts, a former Owens classmate, who after Gissing's death would write his semifictionalized biography, *The Private Life of Henry Maitland* (1912). A noteworthy literary achievement during George's marriage to Nell came with the sale of a novel for cash: "Mrs. Grundy's Enemies" to Bentley for £50. Yet frustratingly for both Gissing and posterity, Bentley became so alarmed at the novel's supposed immorality that he never did issue "Mrs. Grundy," and not even a manuscript has survived. Nevertheless, during these troubled years with Nell, Gissing not only wrote and published *Workers in the Dawn*, but also began the eventually published *Unclassed.* The smallness, however, of his literary earnings forced him to go on tutoring for a livelihood.[28]

By the time of his separation from Nell, Gissing had begun a strangely split existence: days of Grub Street struggle in ugly London rooms but, through his connection with the Harrisons, dinner parties and weekends with the wealthy. Harrison had found Gissing tutorships with such illustrious families as that of Vernon Lushington—a former Secretary to the Admiralty. In particular, one wealthy gentlewoman, Mrs. David Gaussen, treated her children's young tutor as a friend rather than a mere domestic employee. Yet he returned from high society to his humble London niche and a dinner of cold corned beef and ill-cooked potatoes. Once a wealthy lady at a party asked him how he kept his butler in line, and Gissing had to improvise some nonsense about preferring a maid. Even when he moved to less disreputable quarters in order to receive Mrs. Gaussen without shame, his life remained distressingly double.[29] Among well-to-do people, he felt like a social impostor because of his past disgrace. But he yearned to become so famous as a writer that no one would question his background. When *Demos* (1886) sold unusually well, he thought that at last he had gained sufficient fame to enter society safely. He believed that Mrs. Gaussen's praise of *Demos* to all her fashionable acquaintances had raised him in their eyes from an insignificant person to an established man of letters.[30] Yet he remained so much of a social outsider among the well-to-do that Chapman and Hall's manuscript reader, the novelist George Meredith, sensed a basic falsity in Gissing's attempts to portray the rich in fiction. Meredith advised him to stick instead to working-class characters.[31] In actual life, however, Gissing could feel at home neither in low society nor among the high born: he hovered in social limbo.

The limbo was, above all, one of limited sexual choice. In the years of his marriage to Nell, he had lamented the contrast between her alcoholic coarseness and the refinement of the rich young women whom he tutored. With Nell's premature death on 29 February 1888, he found himself wandering between two social worlds—one finished for him but the other frustratingly out of reach. Just one month after Nell's death freed him legally, he rushed down to Eastbourne to court a respectable young Miss Curtis, whom he had apparently met in that seaside town just before the news that his wife had died. Now he plunged into "a long talk with Miss Curtis." In London two weeks later, pacing his "rooms in agony of loneliness," he "thought of Miss Curtis, and longed, longed that she too might have thought of me." He hurried back to Eastbourne to court her again but apparently found a cool welcome: "To Eastbourne—and back. All gone off in smoke. Never mind; the better perhaps." Nell had been dead, at this point, for two months and nine days.[32] Next Gissing fled from his sexual frustration by taking a five-month trip abroad, mainly in Italy, the country of his schoolboy classical dreams. He paid for his unusually long vacation by advance earnings from his newest novel, *The Nether World* (1889). "That is my way," he later explained to a sister, "of making life endurable. Other people have domestic interests. . . . If my life is to be a lonely one, I must travel much. . . .[33] Alone among Roman ruins, he communed with ancient shadows in search of a sexless separate peace.[34] Almost immediately on returning to England, he began another novel to pay for another long trip. Upon finishing *The Emancipated* (1890), he waited to see if his publisher would give him enough for it to support a second excursion into classical lands. When Bentley offered him £150 plus conditional royalties, Gissing at once bought a Baedeker to plan a trip to both Greece and Italy.[35]

But before he could sail, a tantalizing alternative to sexless trips abroad appeared in the person of Edith Sichel, a young English bluestocking. She had sent him a copy of an article of hers discussing his *Demos* (1886) and *Thyrza* (1887). She asked him to her country house in Surrey, where she entertained him pleasantly, although with a chaperone present. She invited him to her London town house, where he decided that "I half think she is beautiful."[36] Miss Sichel's Jewishness may have made her seem accessible to a social outsider like Gissing, yet his discovery that she had an inheritance of £20,000 alarmed as well as attracted him. He had already felt the need to assure her that, although he wrote of the slums, he was no mere untaught workingman.[37] He left on his planned trip with a mind now divided. Gissing "thought much of E[dith] S[ichel]," wrote to her during the first few weeks, and in Athens even dreamed of her:

> A curious and vivid dream last night. Found myself suddenly back in London, and in a room where were present Miss Sichel, . . . Fred. Harrison, and others whom I forget, but whom I knew. I had no recollection of the journey home from Greece, but I was quite conscious that, for whatever reason, I had made it precipitately, and I regretted bitterly having done so. . . . I talked much with Miss Sichel and grew very intimate with her.[38]

By 1889, according to *The Oxford English Dictionary*, *intimate* had become a common euphemism for illicit sexual intercourse. But if the dreaming Gissing yearned for sexual acceptance by the respectable Miss Sichel, he also feared rejection. The dreamer regrets abandoning his consolation trip until he can feel sure of her favor. Soon the waking Gissing began to fidget because she had not answered his letter. Her "reply" came "at last" but seemed so "cold and uninteresting" that he abandoned all hopes about her.[39] Although Gissing continued his solitary trip, it ended badly. He began to suffer from loneliness, and in Naples he developed a "touch" of lung "congestion," the disease that years later would cut short his life.[40]

Back in England he returned to the old Gissing pattern of single-minded fiction writing frequently interrupted by attacks of sexual frustration. Although he now rejected all tutoring in order to work full time on a tentative new novel, he found himself stumbling into many false starts, which he blamed on his lonely state of mind. Once again Gissing seemed to glimpse a chance to marry a respectable young lady. On a visit to his family in Wakefield, he met Connie Ash, a "pretty" friend of his sisters. "I am in love with her, and there's an end of it," he confided to his diary. Nervous but encouraged, he ventured "alone" to the Ashes' house to have a talk with Connie but could not detach her from her sister. "Very shaky and hopeless" in the absence of encouragement, he fled back to London, convinced at last that no eligible Englishwoman would marry an author without lots of money. After thirteen years of authorship and eight published novels, he had won only a small, if discriminating, audience, and he still had to churn out books in rapid succession before he used up money from the last one. The day after Connie had chilled his new hopes, he decided to find instead "some decent" working girl, even though he lacked a specific candidate.[41]

Unhappy Remarriage and Achievement

Experts on Gissing disagree about where, precisely, he found Edith Underwood, his working-class second wife, but one point appears certain: determined as he was to avoid his old mistakes, he did not hunt for her in any red-light district. He may have met her in Marylebone Road, Regent's Park, an Oxford Street café, or the Oxford Music Hall, although clearly not where he told his sister—at a table in Kew Gardens, sipping tea and chaperoned by an Underwood sister and brother.[42] Gissing's Kew story seems false because his *Diary* shows that, in the weeks following the Connie Ash fiasco, he did not go to Kew until he took Edith there four days after first having mentioned her.[43] But his harmless little lie to his sister reveals what he wished to emphasize: (1) Edith drank tea rather than gin; (2) she went to respectable places; (3) she had conventional family ties. In effect, Gissing assured his sister that Edith was no Nell. He insisted on the Underwoods' absolute decency. Edith's father made tombstones, an ignobly decent occupation, but Gissing in his description to his brother embellished Mr. Underwood into a "reputable working-sculptor."[44]

Edith may have turned out somewhat more decent than Gissing had, in fact, bargained for. In his original plan of finding a working girl, he spoke merely of having her "come . . . live with" him. But although Edith often went alone with him to his rooms, he had to admit even four months later that "our relations are as yet platonic. . . . If anything is to come of our connection it will have to be marriage."[45] After several visits by George to Edith's own house with all her family away, her father objected to Gissing's coming. One senses a tug of war between Gissing and the Underwoods. He may have wished for the same tentative arrangement by which he had first lived unmarried with Nell, but this respectable working-class family insisted that he obey the Camden-Town proprieties. At last Gissing gave in. Just after finishing *New Grub Street* (1891), his literary masterpiece, he yielded to the idea of marriage to Edith. Yet once he had realized that her sexual favors could be won only by marrying her, he began to feel serious misgivings. He confessed to his sister that Edith spoke with such a lowbred accent that no other Gissings should see her until he could teach her better English. He would hide her away, he added, from all his circle of friends until he could accustom Edith to the life of the mind. And he thought their planned wedding an absurd formality.[46] When an illness in Edith's family delayed the wedding date, Gissing fired off two successive ultimatums: marry him at once or break off the relationship. He seems to have been groping for a valid excuse to cancel his wedding promise. But instead Edith hastened to marry him on 25 February 1891, and Gissing hurried away with her to Exeter to keep her from both his family and friends.[47]

Although Edith neither worked the streets nor drank and although she at first satisfied his sexual desires, she suited him little more than Nell had, and he cared for Edith much less. For the quick deterioration of their marriage, they seem to share much blame. He clearly neglected this woman for whom he lacked respect, and she responded first with sullenness, then with tantrums, and finally with outright psychotic violence. In their first year together, he rarely mentioned Edith in his diary except to record her illnesses or at last her confinement for pregnancy. The birth of their first child, Walter, on 10 December 1891 only worsened matters, for Edith resented the new maternal duties, and George resented her resentment. Toward the end of their second year, Gissing complained in his diary of Edith's domestic incompetence, her constant quarrels with servants, her crass unintelligence, and her lack of wifely sympathy. Soon his only pleasure in marriage came from his love for his son. In his third married year, Gissing abandoned his plan of retraining Edith in Exeter and moved back to London instead yet still tried to keep her away from most of his family and friends. After three and a half married years, he confessed in his diary that "but for my poor little boy, I would not, and could not, live with her for another day. I have no words for the misery I daily endure from her selfish and coarse nature." In his fifth married year, he began to snatch at opportunities to spend time with literary friends away from Edith's wrangling. By the end of the fifth year, the birth of a second child, Alfred, intensified the couple's quarreling. Three months later Gissing took his now unruly older boy to be brought up by George's sisters, free from the "loveless and utterly unsuitable marriage." By the end of the sixth year, Gissing fell ill with renewed lung trouble. He ran away from Edith's constant bickering, took a three-month lung cure in Devon, but returned to find her acting in alarmingly crazy ways. She began an irrational argument over a missing shaving-brush part, accused him of having hidden it to annoy her, and screamed for him "to hold your beastly noise, or you'll have this plate at your head!" He fled with his bad lungs for a seven-month trip to Italy while his friends in England tried to arrange a legal separation.[48] But Gissing's wish to free himself from Edith appears to have pushed her over the edge of full psychosis. When he returned from abroad to separate lodgings, she "attacked her landlord and his wife with a stick," had to be restrained by a policeman, "destroyed their front garden" in response to being evicted, and threatened Gissing's personal representative. In his final meeting with Edith, on 7 September 1898, Gissing agreed to her keeping the younger boy, provided that her mental health stabilized, and he promised to continue supporting her.[49] Yet less than four years later, Edith's abuse of young Alfred and her menaces against still another landlord led police to take the child away and to commit Edith to a mental hospital. This pathetically disturbed woman remained permanently hospitalized until she died in 1917 of "organic brain disease."[50] In sum, Gissing's second attempt at marriage failed as disastrously as his first.

On top of Edith's upsetting deterioration, Gissing suffered from an increasing awareness that he need not have chosen a working-class wife if only he had waited. Gradually he gained a literary reputation that opened social doors. Indeed, he wrote many of his most important works during this troubled second marriage. He produced such major novels as *Born in Exile* (1892), *The Odd Women* (1893), *In the Year of Jubilee* (1894), and *The Whirlpool* (1897). And he also turned out such fine short stories as "A Victim of Circumstances," "Lou and Liz," "Comrades in Arms," "A Lodger in Maze Pond," "The Poet's Portmanteau," "The Foolish Virgin," "The Schoolmaster's Vision," and "One Way of Happiness."[51]

His income lagged somewhat behind his reputation, but he made at least an adequate living from fiction during this period. *New Grub Street* became his first novel, except for the topical *Demos*, to sell quite well: a second printing within one month, and two subsequent editions within slightly more than a year. But *Born in Exile*, *The Odd Women*, and *In the Year of Jubilee* had disappointingly modest sales. Nevertheless, Clement Shorter, the influential editor of three London journals, admired Gissing's work and asked him for short stories. Soon Gissing depended on his short-story sales for a large part of his earnings. In addition, he churned out quick novelettes that sold rather impressively but sometimes seemed little more than potboilers. Finally, toward the end of his second marriage, he won a truly solid success with *The Whirlpool*: a sale of two thousand copies within the first month, followed by a new printing of another two thousand.[52]

Though he felt ashamed of his wife, Gissing had formed friendships away from his home with distinguished fellow writers: George Meredith, Thomas Hardy, H. G. Wells, James M. Barrie, John Davidson, and numerous others. Gissing also at last found a sympathetic publisher, A. H. Bullen of Lawrence and Bullen, who declared it "a privilege to publish" the novelist's "books." And, frustratingly for Gissing, cultivated women now wanted to make his acquaintance.[53] Yet he remained legally bound to deplorable Edith.

Extralegal "Marriage" and Final Works

Unable to gain the full freedom of divorce after his separation, Gissing still managed to meet Gabrielle Fleury, a French bluestocking who became the third important woman in his life. He attracted her to himself by his considerable literary fame—far greater now than when he had feared that no respectable woman would have him. Gabrielle first visited him in order to ask permission to translate *New Grub Street.* Gissing felt such excitement in at last acting out his dream of winning a lady by his writing that his love letters to Mlle Fleury tend to slip into the verbiage of sentimental bathos.[54] Yet this twenty-nine-year-old Frenchwoman possessed, in fact, those qualities that he had always wanted in a wife: a love of literature, an excellent education, a well-to-do family, an attractive appearance, a pleasant speaking voice, a circle of literary friends, and a deep respect for Gissing's own writings.[55]

Sadly, however, this excellent match had come so very late for Gissing that it had to survive a tangle of complications. Gissing's lung trouble, finally diagnosed as emphysema, grew very serious. Then, too, he could not get a divorce, so that he had to simulate a marriage to Gabrielle in order to protect her reputation. Because a "married" Mlle Fleury could sign neither checks nor documents with her maiden name, she had to transfer her money to be managed by her mother. To George's annoyance, *maman* lived with the couple and became, in effect, the head of the Gissing-Fleury household. Furthermore, this recently widowed mother had such bad heart disease that Gabrielle felt compelled to stay with her in Paris and nurse her, even when George had to leave for lung treatments in somewhat milder regions.[56] Considering these complex troubles, one can hardly wonder that Gissing's extralegal "marriage" did not rise to the heaven of his old erotic daydreams. Yet in spite of "mother-in-law" troubles and his own declining health, Gissing produced two enduring works during his years with Gabrielle: *By the Ionian Sea* (1901) and *The Private Papers of Henry Ryecroft* (1903), plus a number of important Dickens prefaces. He also wrote two of his finest short stories: "The House of Cobwebs" and "A Daughter of the Lodge."

Although his relationship with Gabrielle Fleury seems to have been basically sound, a serious crisis arose in 1901. Gissing visited England with Gabrielle, but, upon her rushing back to nurse her mother, he entered a Suffolk sanatorium for a program of heavy feeding, because, as he claimed, his "mother-in-law" had "starved" him with skimpy French meals. His "wife" complained bitterly about this two-month separation. Yet a few months after his return to France, when his Paris doctor sent him for his health to Arcachon, Gabrielle, instead of nursing *him*, remained glued to *maman*, who resisted leaving Paris. In short, the central problem in this extralegal "marriage" seems to have come from a "wife's" divided loyalty between mother and "husband," which made George complain that Gabrielle was no "wife" at all but a mere "*garde-malade*" for her mother. Gabrielle herself finally settled the issue by persuading her mother to move where Gissing had to live—to southwestern France. Reunited at Saint-Jean-de-Luz and then at Saint-Jean-Pied-de-Port, George and Gabrielle spent eighteen months together in perhaps the happiest span of his life. In a relatively calm domestic haven, he continued writing steadily until his untimely death, on 28 December 1903, from congested lungs and myocarditis.[57]

Chapter Two

Working-Class Novels

Gissing first won widespread attention with his proletarian novels. Yet, in 1897, long after he had given up writing them, he confessed that "the working class . . . for the purposes of fiction . . . is . . . still waiting its portrayer; much has been written about it in novels, but we have no work of the first order dealing primarily with that form of life."[1] By implication, that judgment includes five of his own novels: *Workers in the Dawn*, *The Unclassed*, *Demos*, *Thyrza*, and *The Nether World.* Except for *The Nether World*, Gissing's working-class books do not stand among his own best productions. Still, the very absence of first-rate Victorian novels about proletarian life makes Gissing's earnest efforts important. P. J. Keating has noted how Victorian writers tended to "idealize" their working-class heroes and heroines, to present them as exceptional or, in actuality, as middle-class exemplars transparently disguised by overalls or smocks.[2] Although Gissing's stories of the laboring poor never wholly abandoned "idealism" and romance, he began to undercut them by a growing insistence that no one, however splendid, could escape the ill effects of poverty-ridden neighborhoods and cultural deprivations.

Realism versus Idealism

According to the *Oxford English Dictionary*, *romance* means "a fictitious narrative in prose of which the scene and incidents are very remote from those of ordinary life," but *realism* implies "fidelity of representation" to just such ordinary incidents and scenes. Yet from the novel's beginnings to Gissing's own time, many so-called "realists" peopled ordinary fictional neighborhoods with impossibly noble characters. Thus, the "idealizing" tendency of romances influenced allegedly "realistic" novels. By the eighteenth century, this trend expressed itself in the movement known as *sentimentalism*, epitomized by the father of the English novel, Samuel Richardson (1689–1761); in *Clarissa* (1748) and in *Sir Charles Grandison* (1754), he depicted the emotional benevolence of soulful heroines and heroes. By the early nineteenth century, however, the label of *sentimental* had received a bad name from such best-selling appeals to the handkerchief and the heart as the notorious and anonymous *Fatherless Fanny* (1818). Most nineteenth-century portrayers of elevated souls preferred to adopt the term *idealism* from the German philosophic movement started by Immanuel Kant (1724–1804), which stressed ideas rather than concrete objects in interpreting human experience. Among early-Victorian novelists, Edward Bulwer-Lytton (1803–1873) most eloquently defended what Gissing would later call the "poor stuff" of "idealism" (see above, "Preface"). Bulwer urged fellow writers not to copy living individuals, but to express "a certain nobleness of sentiment, which, however modified, exists in every genuinely noble nature."[3]

This "idealizing" strain within a "realistic" genre has important connections with the moralistic assumption that novels should improve their readers—in short, with a pervasive Victorian didacticism that one might call neo-Neoclassic. But this nineteenth-century literary insistence that fiction teach morality also connects with religious evangelicalism: a widespread Victorian emphasis upon moral conduct as the alpha and omega of the Christian faith. During this age, critics, as well as publishers' readers, tended to praise or blame fictional characters for their moral uplift or downdraft. Thus, in the early 1880s, Gissing himself ran afoul of a censorious late-Victorian publisher; George Bentley at first accepted the writer's now-lost novel "Mrs. Grundy's Enemies" but later refused to issue it. Bentley changed his mind because of an editor's warning that the book's most ignoble characters received too little blame and that the work as a whole gave inadequate answers to pressing social questions.[4] Here, apparently, the problem arose less from the absence of didacticism than from what Bentley considered the wrong didactic stress—a rejection of accepted social morality.

Gissing himself noted, however, that his great predecessor Dickens welcomed Victorian moral uplift and became its chief spokesman (see below, Chap. 9). Indeed, Dickens's popular didacticism provided the basic tradition from which Gissing began and against which he later rebelled. Through what Louis Cazamian has called "the philosophy of Christmas," Dickens proclaimed his era's optimistic faith in benevolent philanthropy and social reform.[5]

Gissing's early novels contain similar idealizations of noble philanthropists, qualified, however, by some un-Dickensian doubts about the ultimate practicality of their schemes: Mr. Tollady and Helen Norman in *Workers in the Dawn* (1880), Ida Starr in *The Unclassed* (1884), and Walter Egremont in *Thyrza* (1887). But Gissing's early fiction also stresses two completely un-Dickensian "ideals": moral-aesthetic paragons who love high culture, and sexual partners who excel in courtly graces. Significantly, both the art-for-art's-sakers and the love-for-love's-sakers contradict high Victorian didacticism by exalting private experience over public duty. Yet the youthful Gissing insists upon the genuine "idealism" of these artists and lovers as well as of his selfless philanthropists.

Beginning with his very first novel, Gissing specifically invokes the word *ideal* to extol his heroine's virtues. But in *The Unclassed*, *ideal* and its variants appear still more frequently, as Gissing praises his two rival heroines. *Demos* (1886) makes an even more insistent use of *idealism* and *ideal* in order to laud both courtly love and high artistic taste. By the time of *Thyrza*, *ideal*, *idealist*, and *idealism* recur in dozens of disquisitions on philanthropy, love, and art. Initially, Gissing actually planned to call his novel "The Idealist"—the eventual title of *Thyrza*'s second chapter. But after he had written an unsatisfactory draft of *The Nether World*'s chapter xii, Gissing lost his appetite for "all this idealism."[6] Whatever that chapter may originally have contained, its scornful final version attacks the hope that poverty-stricken humans can find redemption through philanthropy, love, or art. Although *The Nether World* as a whole retains significant traces of Christmas benevolence, courtly romance, and even high aestheticism, these "ideals" have now become problems instead of solutions. Ultimately, the book's characters learn the irrelevance of sublime aspirations within an impoverished and brutalized environment.

Workers in the Dawn

In *Workers in the Dawn* (1880), a potentially effective realistic story drawn from private experience struggles to break away from the surrounding conventions of sentimental and melodramatic fiction. The embedded story approximates Gissing's own difficult life with Nell. Arthur Golding (Gissing with three letters changed) takes pity on a seduced and abandoned young girl whom he finds freezing to death on a snow-covered London street. He marries her, only to discover that she has become alcoholic and has turned to prostitution for brandy money. After many frustrated attempts to reform her, he packs his bags in the night, runs away to America, and finally throws himself into Niagara Falls. The strength of the Arthur-Carrie sequence lies in the pathetic portrayal of the alcoholic prostitute, with her flat simple speech and her limited intelligence, and not in the indulgent self-projection of the Gissing-Golding character, who supposedly burns with true creative genius. In any case, the Carrie Mitchell story takes up only eleven of forty-seven chapters, or less than one-fourth of this sprawling book.

The rest of *Workers* mixes realism and idealism in jarringly incongruous ways. In the pagination of the 1935 edition,[7] the first 122 pages give a neo-Dickensian account of Arthur Golding's orphaned childhood, as he bounces back and forth from wicked oppressors to sunny Good Samaritans: a vicious London landlady, an elegant country clergyman, a kindly rural family, a sadistic London beggar, a friendly Cockney potato vender, a gruff owner of a big-city pet shop, and a saintly but poor master printer named

Tollady. Next the book shuttles between parallel narratives of high and low life: poverty-stricken Arthur struggles on as a painter-printer-philanthropist, and Helen Norman, the clergyman's daughter, marches toward moral, intellectual, and philanthropic perfection. Arthur and Helen converge in a tentative romance but get separated by assorted complications, climaxed by the stagy jealousy of her guardian. Not only do the high-life characters seem mere bookish fantasies, but Gissing attaches them to Arthur's squalid adventures with traditional all-purpose novelistic glue: a legacy from Helen's father splices Arthur into fashionable life.

We must wait till page 428 for the Carrie Mitchell story. And Gissing weakens even it by making Carrie the sexual rival of a daydream Helen Norman. As Gillian Tindall has noted, Gissing christened his "ideal" with the middle name of his actual prostitute companion—Marianne Helen (Nell) Harrison.[8] Obviously, he made Helen a wish fulfillment—a Nell turned into saint—but he drew Carrie from the brawling living woman. This juxtaposition of seraph and slut transforms Arthur's marital dilemma into conventional melodrama. When Carrie runs off, he contemplates bigamy with the unknowing angel, Helen. When he tries again to reclaim his drunken wife, he acts only at Helen's noble bidding. And when he finally kills himself, he does so simply because seraphic Helen has died.

Gissing further compromises the realism of *Workers in the Dawn* by aiming at a localized decorum, a separation of styles within a single page or even a single paragraph. He uses low prose for slum dwellers and elevated verbosity for gentlefolk. These stylistic shifts involve much more than merely adjusting speeches to a character's debasement or altitude. When dealing with high, low, or middle-level characters, the narrative voice itself rises, falls, or steadies. Erich Auerbach has shown that literary realism requires "complete emancipation" from "the classical rule of distinct levels of style."[9] Although Gissing mixes styles within his novel, he usually attempts a rigid distinction between prose used for social depths and prose saved for the heights.

Workers in the Dawn contains three contrasting manners: a low style that struggles against the author's persistent hankering for Latinate ornateness; a high style drawn from "silver-fork" romances; and, most successfully, a plain style for plain people and things. Consider this opening description of Mr. Norman's entrance into Adam and Eve Court:

> At length, having entered a small shop to make inquiries, he crossed the road, and after some hesitation, was turning into a narrow, loathsome alley, which the light of a street lamp showed, bore the name of Adam and Eve Court, when a little girl, suddenly rushing out of the darkness, bumped unawares against him and fell to the ground, breaking to pieces a jug which she held in her hands. She did not begin to cry, but, instantly springing to her feet, proceeded to assail the cause of her accident with a stream of the foulest abuse, which would have been dreadful enough on the lips of a grown-up man, but appeared unutterably so as coming from a child.
>
> "You've broke the jug, you have!" screamed the little creature at last, having exhausted her epithets; "you've broke the jug, you have; and you'll 'ave to pay for it, you will. Come, now, pay for the jug, will you, mister?"
>
> "Good God!" exclaimed the gentleman, half to himself, "what a hell I have got into!" (I, pt. I, ch. i, 9)

The prose becomes concrete and simple only after the slum girl darts onto the page. Gissing's plain words for her movements—"suddenly rushing," "bumped unawares," "fell to the ground," "breaking to pieces a jug"—contrast with the stiff language used for Mr. Norman: "at length," "to make inquiries," "after some hesitation." Even the furious single-mindedness of the child's staccato repetitions—"broke the jug, you have," "broke the jug, you have," "pay for it, you will," "pay for the jug, will you"—clashes with the preceding overloaded sentences, those loose, unemphatic strings of subordinate clauses and modifying phrases. And the central action, the smashing of the jug, gets shunted into a mere participal phrase. Perhaps most significantly, the passage's expressions of fastidious disgust come not only from the "gentleman," but also from the gentlemanly narrator: "loathsome," "the foulest abuse," "dreadful enough," "unutterably so." In the previous six pages, he has invited his reader to "walk with" him through this Cockney slum, at which he flings Latinate scoldings: "unspeakable abominations," "foul-mouthed virulence," "a torrent of inanity, abomination, and horrible blasphemy which bespeaks the very depth of human—aye, or of bestial—degradation" (I, pt. I, ch. i, 3, 4, 7). The pomposity of invective suggests an underlying personal need: to establish the author's own gentlemanliness in spite of his lower-class subject.

A similar motive probably explains the narrator's sudden shifts to pseudoaristocratic prose. Take this typically stilted sentence about the man who later becomes Helen Norman's guardian: "Mr. Gilbert Gresham was a man of some thirty-six years of age, of tall and well-proportioned figure, and blessed with features, to adopt the easily-comprehended phrase, of an aristocratic cast" (I, pt. I, ch. x, 138). Notice all the "elegant variations" packed into one clause: "of some thirty-six years of age" = thirty-six years old; "of tall and well-proportioned figure" = tall and thin; blessed with features . . . of an aristocratic cast" = aristocratic looking. Then, too, the parenthetical "to adopt the easily comprehended phrase" tries to assure the reader that both he and the novelist know all about aristocratic faces.

On the other hand, the most effective passages in *Workers* have a plain force like the blunt speeches given to Carrie. Consider the following scene where Arthur fetches her back in spite of her sordid debauches:

> Beckoning her to follow, he pushed open the door and entered. In a few moments he had paid for a night's lodging, and, accompanied by Carrie, was shown upstairs into a small and not too clean-looking bedroom. The waiter gave him a candle and retired. Arthur turned the key in the door, and then faced Carrie, whose eyes had followed his motions with wonder. . . .
>
> ". . . Have you still any love for me, Carrie?"
>
> "I have always loved you," she said, weeping bitterly. "It isn't you as has been cruel to me, Arthur; it's me as has behaved as if I hated you, though all the while I loved you better than I ever loved any one

else. It was all the drink; it drove me to do things and to say things as I shouldn't never have thought on, and I didn't mean—no, upon my word, I didn't. If I can only keep from drink, Arthur, I could be a faithful and hard-working wife, indeed I could. I'll do my best, I will. But I feel I'm not fit to live with you. I never was fit." (II, pt. III, ch. xiv, 384–85)

Compared with the opening scene about the Reverend Mr. Norman, this one has a unified tone. Both the narrator and Carrie stick to simple words: he, to describe actions and things; she, to express feelings. Although he complicates his sentences slightly more than Carrie's by using modifying phrases to express simultaneity—"beckoning her to follow" and "accompanied by Carrie"—he keeps his basic units almost as short as hers. The similarities appear far more decisive than the differences. The chief stylistic contrast arises from Carrie's repetition of "I," "I," "I," "it," "it," "it," but this goes with excited speech as opposed to calm narration. And Gissing minimizes a potential shift in style by limiting Carrie's uneducated diction mainly to one small repeated error—"as" misused for *that*—plus a single "on" for *of*, and the double negative "shouldn't never." Her dialect seems mild compared with the Cockneyisms of other working-class characters, such as chapter one's nasty landlady: "If anythink 'appens to him, sir (which, and I'm sure, I 'ope as it won't) . . ." (I, pt. I, ch. ii, 11). Significantly, both the narrator and Carrie stress the paltry contradictions inherent in the scene. He undercuts the emotions of the reunion by noting the "not too clean-looking bedroom." And she undercuts her excuse of "drink" by confessing that "I never was fit." Here, in scattered pages, lie hints of Gissing's later strength—the depiction of poor but fastidious characters who must express their sensitivity against a squalid backdrop.

The Unclassed

As the title of *The Unclassed* (1884) suggests, this book resists the simple category of working-class fiction. Yet because of the important role played by the London slum background, Gissing's second book has more in common with *Workers in the Dawn*, *Demos*, *Thyrza*, and *The Nether World* than with his middle-class novels. In *The Unclassed* the slums provide a menacing boundary beyond the central figures' tenuous respectability. Gissing himself, however, later pointed out the book's hybrid nature, for he argued in the preface to his 1895 revision that *The Unclassed* contains more "romance" than realism and that "all the prominent persons of the story dwell in a limbo external to society."[10]

The novel's opening scene shows the three female protagonists as rather young girls in a northwest-London school: naive Ida Starr has struck Harriet Smales with a slate for maliciously but truthfully calling Ida's mother a prostitute, and Ida's wistful friend, Maud Enderby, has witnessed the attack. Just when Ida gets expelled from school, her mother falls fatally ill. The dying mother asks her own wooden-hearted father, appropriately named Woodstock, to take in the child. But having long ago driven his daughter into prostitution, he now fails to save his granddaughter.

Eight years later a friendship develops between Osmond Waymark and Julian Casti, the two men who will involve themselves with the book's three major females. The struggling novelist Waymark feels sexually attracted first to Maud and then to Ida, as they alternately pop in and out of his life. Although Maud seems outwardly a lady, she has an embezzler father, a psychotic mother, and a bizarrely overreligious guardian-aunt. Although Ida has become a prostitute, she remains essentially an ingenue. Meanwhile, the would-be writer Casti is tricked into marriage by despicable Harriet Smales, who possesses an unaccountable taste for the company of barmaids and other low women.

By a series of coincidences, Waymark takes a job collecting slum rents for Ida's cold-hearted grandfather, who has lost all track of her. Ida soon gives up prostitution for work in a laundry, in order to win Waymark's approval, but he has already involved himself with Maud. In an effort to relieve Casti's marital troubles, Waymark suggests that Ida attempt to befriend the jealous and spiteful Harriet. Harriet, however, rigs false evidence to send Ida to jail for a theft that she never committed. With Ida imprisoned, the hero becomes engaged to Maud. Then, just before the morning of Ida's release, a slum-dwelling robber ties up Waymark and thus prevents him from meeting the martyred heroine outside the prison gates. In his frustration and anguish, he decides that he really loves the noble ex-prostitute rather than the ladylike Maud. Meanwhile Woodstock has found and befriended his long-lost granddaughter, and the now-remorseful old man sets her up in comfort. But although she uses his slum-begotten money for philanthropy among the poor, Woodstock has repented too late: he dies from typhus caught while inspecting his dilapidated houses. In a last twist of the subplot, Casti runs away from his contemptible wife but dies of tuberculosis brought on by marital suffering. Out of hysterical asceticism, Maud finally renounces her engagement to Waymark and thus frees him to marry Ida, the reformed ex-prostitute, and live happily ever after.

The novel's most impressive parts foreshadow *New Grub Street* by depicting the lives of poor but literate men on the edges of working-class squalor. Literacy raises these "unclassified" males above the surrounding proletariat, although, in Waymark's case, his novelistic gifts also help focus his understanding of proletarian hardships. Literacy itself and a taste for high culture provide a certain respectability even within the worst hovels. Appropriately, then, Gissing introduces his "unclassed" characters with sociological descriptions not only of their shabby dwellings, but also of their books and prints. Waymark, for example, lives squalidly enough in "not too clean, generally uninviting" lodgings, but he owns volumes of literature "reaching from floor to ceiling" and "pictures of other than the lodging-house type" (ch. vi, 41, 42). Casti lives above a chemist's shop in an inexpensive bedroom that must double as his "sitting-room," yet his bookcases are packed with "Latin poets, . . . Italian books," and also "English classics." Even Casti's humble walls display impressive engravings of "ancient and modern" Rome (ch. vi, 40). By contrast, the narrative's archetypal slum dweller, the animalistic Slimy, has debased his already sordid room with his own repulsive graffiti: "The walls were all scribbled over with obscene words and drawings" ch. xii,

100–1). Although Gissing concedes that Slimy has suffered degradation through social forces beyond his control, the juxtaposition of poetry with mere scrawled-out lewdness, of classical engravings with crude dirty pictures, dramatizes the need for culture's saving graces even within the slums.

Unlike *New Grub Street*, however, *The Unclassed* portrays its poor but literate women with far less verisimilitude than it brings to its men. Compared to Waymark and Casti, Ida Starr remains pretty much a fantasy—a dream triumph of bookishness over prostitution. At first her fallen mother grooms little Ida to become a respectable teacher by enrolling her in a better-than-average school (ch. i, 3; ch. iii, 23–24). But the mother's own disinterest in the world of books prevents the child from liking them, and, in any case, Ida's formal education soon ends with expulsion (ch. ii, 14–15; ch. iii, 24). Yet after becoming a prostitute at only seventeen (ch. xi, 90; ch. xvii, 140), she develops an unlikely hunger for serious literature. Using Waymark as her own private lending library and also as her tutor, she borrows copies of *Jane Eyre* and other classics, and they read them together (ch. xiv, 110; ch. xix, 160–62; ch. xxii, 181). Ultimately, she even takes formal lessons in order to become worthy of the hero (ch. xxxi, 254). And when he fails to send her his recently published novel, she buys it herself, reads it, and praises it to him (ch. xxxvi, 294–95). In this wish-fulfilling dream, the ex-prostitute emerges not only as the writer-hero's ideal love, but also as his ideal reader.

Gissing also idealizes Maud Enderby. If she undergoes an allegorical struggle between ascetic Christianity and secular art, she has all the graces of a courtly heroine. Though Maud grows up in a grim evangelical home filled with pious reproductions of Christ's agony (ch. iv, 32–33), she becomes what Ida unsuccessfully aimed at—a teacher of secular culture (ch. viii, 62–64). Through Waymark, Maud learns to love nonreligious literature—specifically Rossetti's erotic poems (ch. xxvi, 217; ch. xxvii, 221, 223). But her final rejection of art for fanatical asceticism reveals her incompatability with Gissing's writer-protagonist (ch. xxxvii, 305–6).

Unlike the idealized Maud and Ida, the book's third major female, the villainous Harriet Smales, has a grubby circumstantiality. But Gissing's uncontrolled hatred of this figure tends to reduce her to caricature. Symptomatically, she despises both literature and art until her dying day. Like Ida's mother, Harriet's father wishes that his child might become a teacher. But he rightly fears that she lacks the brains for such intellectual work (ch. iv, 31). Harriet herself sees no point at all in Casti's efforts to write great literature (ch. ix, 69). Instead of the classics, she reads penny weeklies, and she models her sleazy efforts to ensnare her male victim upon stereotyped fictional trash (ch. xiii, 102). With still greater boorishness, Harriet shows annoyance whenever Casti himself reads his beloved works of literature (ch. xx, 163). As the climax of her philistinism, she burns a poem that her husband has just written (ch. xxxv, 282). But the novel's last chapter takes fictional revenge upon this enemy of literature: Gissing has Harriet fall "downstairs in a fit" and break "her neck" (ch. xxxviii, 312). This ultimate punishment foreshadows his praise of Dickens's fictional method for chastizing the ill-tempered Mrs. Gargery in *Great Expectations* (1860–1861): ". . . a half-murderous blow on the back of her head from which she will never recover. . . . There is no other efficacious way with these ornaments of their sex. A felling and stunning and all but killing blow, followed by paralysis and slow death. A sharp remedy, but no whit sharper than the evil it cures."[11] Before Gissing could write his best novels, he had to cease portraying women as either book-hating devils or high aesthetic angels.

Demos

Demos (1886) creates anti-Socialist propaganda out of Gissing's own private obsessions about status and class. Published anonymously in the first edition, the book exploits Britain's mid-decade fear of Socialist revolution. Made topical by the Trafalgar Square riot of 1886, this polemical novel sold far better than the author's earlier books.[12] Because of its snobbish disdain for the working classes and its idealization of gentlefolk, *Demos* now seems more dated than Gissing's major works. Yet the writer's own yearning for an upwardly mobile marriage gives an intermittent power to this cautionary tale of a Socialist who marries a lady.[13]

Demos begins just after the death of old Mr. Mutimer, a wealthy mine owner. His apparent failure to leave a will disinherits his expected heir, young Hubert Eldon, a proud but landless aristocrat. Instead the wealth goes to young Richard Mutimer, a working-class Socialist. In addition to gaining Eldon's expected legacy, young Mutimer also wins the aristocrat's sweetheart, the genteel Adela Waltham, after her mother has convinced the girl of Eldon's sexual sins. In order to marry this fashionable young lady, Mutimer discards his working-class fiancée, the humble Emma Vine. He vows to devote his mining profits to the Socialist cause but displays hypocrisy in his socialism. As a further complication, Mutimer and his relatives cannot adjust to Adela's genteel world. By now disillusioned with her working-class husband, Adela finds a lost will that leaves the estate to Eldon after all. Then this Socialist-hating hero shuts down the mine and restores the valley to its lyrical state of green. The working-class protagonist, however, receives an unexpected annuity from a Socialist admirer to finance work for the cause. But Mutimer foolishly sinks his own savings and those of his fellow workers in a fraudulent corporation that promises high dividends. When the company director absconds, Mutimer has to defend his own honesty before an angry proletarian mob that eventually assaults him. He dies in the forgiving presence of angelic Emma Vine, the working girl whom he jilted. As the novel closes, Adela and Eldon plan to marry and live happily ever after.

Demos's polemic sting comes from Gissing's depiction of even a "labor aristocrat" as a crude and bungling opportunist. The narrator explicitly describes Mutimer—a mechanical engineer—as an exceptional workingman who exemplifies "the best qualities his class can show."[14] In an essay on the "labor aristocracy," E. J. Hobsbawm has stressed the job skills of this upper-working-class stratum, its comparatively high literacy rate, and its overall sense of superiority to the proletarian masses.[15] But Gissing concedes Mutimer's virtues as a "labor aristocrat" only to expose them as woefully inadequate for life among cultivated gentlefolk.

Although Gissing's exceptional workingman begins with a proud "consciousness of his points of superiority to the men among whom he lived" (ch. iv, 33), he ends by confessing his unworthiness of the genteel Adela. Indeed, he finally wishes that he "had been brought up in the same kind of way that you [Adela] were—that's the difference between us, you see" (ch. xxxv, 449). Removed from his proper sphere, this exemplary workingman becomes an incompetent capitalist, a fiancée deserter, and an insensitive husband. Characteristically, however, Gissing blames Mutimer's subsequent faults upon his original lack of culture and of high aesthetic training. Thus, his library contains only outdated radical polemics: "English literature was to him a sealed volume; poetry he scarcely knew by name; of history he was worse than ignorant . . ." (ch. v, 42).

Mutimer's ill-bred sister, Alice, has even less taste than he does. Before the inheritance, she reads only the most vulgar penny-paper fiction; afterwards she reads equally vulgar circulating-library novels (ch. ix, 110). And Mutimer's younger brother "'Arry," an uncouth drain-pipe clerk (ch. iii, 30), amounts to little more than an *h*-dropping imitation of an actual cartoon "'Arry"—E. J. Milliken's satirical drawings of a working-class upstart with flashy bad taste.[16] Gissing extends full sympathy only to lower-class characters who maintain a respectful distance from cultivated persons. He deals gently, for example, with Mutimer's lowly mother because she disapproves "of a workin' man's children goin' to live in big 'ouses" (ch. xxxi, 409). In addition, the novelist depicts jilted Emma Vine as a working-class saint who accepts the vast gulf between her humble self and the poetry-loving seraph Adela (ch. xxxvi, 472).

Gissing's idealizing aestheticism particularly weakens *Demos*'s portraits of cultivated gentlefolk. Through an exalted discovery of literature, music, and art, Adela becomes transformed from a merely genteel ingenue to a "high-hearted" and cultivated paragon (ch. xxi, 281, 286, 288–89; ch. xxvi, 346). Eldon shows his moral right to vast inherited wealth by becoming an esteemed art critic (ch. xxi, 290–91). On the other hand, the minor character Westlake, a fictional travesty of William Morris (1834–1896), deserts great poetry for Socialist agitation and thus betrays his art: "His very style has abandoned him," Eldon complains: "his English smacks of the street corners, of Radical clubs. The man is ruined . . ." (ch. xxix, 381). Gissing gives aestheticism the ultimate triumph as Eldon demolishes the Socialist's mines and remakes the valley into a natural work of art for the happy few who appreciate beauty (ch. xxvi, 338–39; ch. xxxvi, 461–62). Surrounded by this idealized version of high culture, even crude and blundering Mutimer commands from the reader a certain comparative sympathy—a sympathy that subverts the book's anti-Socialist theme.

Thyrza

Although *Thyrza* (1887) presents its working-class characters with far more sympathy than *Demos*, Gissing exempts his hat-trimmer heroine from proletarian manners by giving her an "artist's soul."[17] If the secondary characters seem convincingly working class, Thyrza herself is consistently sentimentalized. Gillian Tindall has described this gifted virginal heroine as a wish-fulfilling apotheosis of Gissing's own Nell—a Nell the prostitute gone impossibly right.[18] Reflecting the author's 1880s aestheticism, Thyrza undergoes an operatic transformation—*operatic* in the figurative sense but also literally *operatic*: the once lowly seamstress takes classical singing lessons.

As the story opens, the verse-writing Walter Egremont explains an idealistic project to the wealthy Newthorpe family. He plans to give literary lectures to artisans from his late father's south-London factory. After Egremont announces this scheme, he proposes marriage to Annabel Newthorpe, a well-read young lady, but she gently turns him down. Meanwhile, in the Lambeth district where the hero will deliver his lectures, beautiful Thyrza

Trent lives with her plain but good-hearted sister, Lydia. Thyrza herself captivates two superior artisans who later attend Egremont's cultural sessions: Luke Ackroyd, adored by Lydia but not by Thyrza, and Gilbert Grail, a book-loving candle-maker with Gissing's own initials. Rejected by Thryza, Ackroyd ignores Lydia and instead switches his affection to Totty Nancarrow, an irrepressible neighborhood hoyden. At the same time, Egremont appoints Grail librarian of a new working-class library, and the candle-maker at last proposes to Thyrza and becomes formally engaged to her. Yet she and Egremont meet, quickly fall in love, and carry on a secret flirtation. Although the hero tries to resist his passion and finally hurries abroad to avoid wronging Grail, the broken-hearted Thyrza flees her unglamorous fiancé and disappears mysteriously from Lambeth. Scandalous rumors about Thyrza and Egremont force Grail to resign his librarianship, thus ending his patron's philanthropic schemes.

From this point on, Gissing elevates Thyrza into an idealized aesthetic angel. In broken health, she takes secret refuge with a matronly friend of Egremont's, one Mrs. Ormonde, who unintentionally becomes the villainess. Because she wants Egremont to marry Annabel Newthorpe—his former love—Mrs. Ormonde makes him wait two whole years before proposing to Thyrza. The girl, however, overhears Mrs. Ormonde's crucial interview with the hero. As a result, Thyrza works contentedly at becoming a concert singer worthy of Egremont's love. Yet when he returns after his cooling-off period and learns that she has lived happily without him, he feels no need to propose. The despairing heroine now agrees to a loveless marriage with Grail. But she dies first from a disease well known to lovers of grand opera—sentimental cardiac arrest. And Gissing underscores her saintly apotheosis by having her die at a moment of empathetic joy over her sister's belated engagement to Ackroyd. In a final tying up of romantic odds and ends, Totty Nancarrow marries an artisan named Bunce, and Egremont settles for marrying Annabel Newthorpe.

Although *Thyrza* represents an advance for Gissing in the sympathetic portrayal of working-class life, his insistence on his heroine's great artistic soul, his obsession with Grail's and Egremont's high aesthetic standards, seem discordantly bookish intrusions into the artisan milieu. Egremont himself enters Lambeth to preach love of literature. Grail makes worshipful trips to the writers' tombs in Westminster Abbey (ch. iii, 23; ch. vi, 62–63). He regards with "bliss unutterable" his appointment as Egremont's librarian: "Books, books, and time to use them, and a hearth about which love is busy—what more can you offer son of man than these?" (ch. xii, 144). Grail courts Thyrza by lending her a life of Thomas More (ch. vi, 64). Egremont flirts with her as they unpack books in the library and chat about an eight-volume Gibbon (ch. xix, 214–17). And during Egremont's absence abroad, the heroine strives to become truly worthy of him by studying world history "till midnight" with the help of her trusty dictionary (ch. xxxiii, 397–98).

Thyrza's finest working-class scenes stand apart from all this bookishness. Indeed, the two most impressive working-class characters undergo no aesthetic improvement at all during the novel's course: Luke Ackroyd chooses applied science over literature (ch. xxxiv, 406–10), and Totty Nancarrow prefers marmalade, pickles, and music-hall nights to evenings of studious reading (ch. xxxii, 383–85). In one key chapter, Gissing describes sympathetically an artisans' "friendly lead"—a musical benefit for a disabled barber—which illustrates their cheerful solidarity against common economic hardships (ch. iv). Because Gissing softens his usual scornful comments about Cockney lowness, he manages to portray the vitality of proletarian culture.

A perceptive twentieth-century analyst of working-class life, Richard Hoggart, thinks the early 1880s (the years described by *Thyrza*) the beginning of "the finest period in English urban popular song."[19] In depicting the "friendly lead," Gissing stresses the good-humored Cockney banter but also the pathos of the lyrics: a sad "ditty" about a girl lost in the snow, a lament about unrequited love in " 'Ol-lo-w'y," and a "ballad" about "springtime" in "the country" sung by an overworked factory girl. She would, the narrator comments, "struggle on as long as any one would employ her, then ... fall among the forgotten wretched. And she sang of May-bloom and love; ... sang, with her eyes upon the beer-stained table, in a public-house amid the backways of Lambeth" (ch. iv, 39–43). With a tolerance often lacking in his earlier working-class fiction, Gissing perceives Cockney music and jokes as triumphs over squalid surroundings. If he brings the scene to a climax by presenting Thyrza herself as an outright musical genius transcending Cockney art, he also describes the crowd's delight at her uncommon voice (ch. iv, 44). The entire chapter does more to evoke a vital working-class culture than all of Egremont's sermons about great books for artisans.

The Nether World

With *The Nether World* (1889), Gissing achieved his finest portrayal of working-class life—indeed one of the finest in the Victorian novel.[20] The book stresses its characters' nightmarish entrapment in poverty-stricken surroundings. Gissing's indignant pity goes far beyond the off-and-on compassion of his earlier proletarian fiction, partly because *The Nether World* excludes all high-life digressions. Yet the novel's exceptional working-class hero and heroine preserve, in muted form, much of Gissing's earlier idealism: a love of art, an urge toward philanthropy, a belief in the perfect mate. Here, however, idealism becomes a handicap of the sensitive, unfitting them to compete for petty advantages among degraded slum proletarians.

As *The Nether World* begins, the secret bearer of inherited wealth, old Michael Snowdon, enters a grim East London slum in search of his granddaughter Jane. Motherless and abandoned by her father, Jane Snowdon lives tormented by callous employers—Mrs. Peckover and her sadistic daughter Clem. Sidney Kirkwood, the jeweler-assistant hero, befriends thirteen-year-old Jane but has already fallen in love with Clara Hewett, a working-class beauty who aims at more than a mere artisan husband. When Clara runs away from her family and acquaintances, her doting father, John, blames Sidney. Clara, however, seeks to become a professional actress by bartering away her sexual favors to a man who can help her. Meanwhile, her brother Bob, a knavish die-sinker who will soon become a counterfeiter, marries Penelope ("Pennyloaf") Candy, a pathetic working drudge. And John Hewett succumbs to deepest despair and poverty. Jane, however, finds refuge with her secretly rich grandfather, comforts poor "Pennyloaf," and becomes Sidney's soul mate. But Jane's long-vanished father, Joseph Snowdon, suddenly reappears, and this unscrupulous man marries Clem, his own daughter's bitterest enemy, and schemes to win old Snowdon's fortune.

At last, Sidney confesses his love for the now-grown-up Jane. As a result, old Snowdon reveals his wealth and also his philanthropic wish that Jane use it all for the poor and not herself. To avoid seeming to crave money, the unworldly hero now balks at actually proposing to Jane. At this point, Clara Hewett unexpectedly reappears. On the very verge of theatrical success, she has suffered facial disfigurement from an acid-flinging attack by a rival actress. Clara, nevertheless, returns to her father's house and manipulates Sidney into proposing marriage in spite of her hideous scars. Before Jane hears this news, she has already experienced distress at her grandfather's new demand that she stay unmarried for the sake of her philanthropic duties. Her resultant fainting fit softens him, however, and he burns his philanthropic will. Yet when Sidney tells her of his impending marriage to Clara, Jane asks old Snowdon to restore her charitable fund. But before he can, he dies intestate and thus permits his son to inherit all the wealth. As the novel closes, Sidney struggles to support his complaining wife and his poverty-stricken in-laws. Rejecting an allowance from her dishonest father, Jane returns to humble labor, but she manages to comfort poor "Pennyloaf," whose counterfeiting husband has died in the hands of the police. Finally, Jane's father dies abroad after losing all his riches, and the separated hero and heroine live unhappily but bravely ever after.

For the first time in Gissing's proletarian fiction, neither artistic creativity nor idealized sexual love enables his protagonists to distance themselves from debasing urban squalor. If Jane and

Sidney preserve certain idealized virtues of Gissing's earlier heroines and heroes, these now-ineffectual sublimities cannot overcome the "nether-world's" ferocity. Although Sidney as a child showed talent for drawing, his own indolence and his father's bankruptcy had kept the would-be artist in a merely servile trade (ch. vi, 52). Years later, when the artisan-hero again tries to draw, a few discouraging visits to London art galleries convince him that he lacks the genius to transcend proletarian life (ch. vi, 58). Sidney's final attempt at sketching occurs during a brief rural vacation with Jane and Michael Snowdon, away from the "city of the damned" (ch. xix, 164; ch. xx, 170). But the hero's aesthetic idealism leaves him utterly defenseless against those who care for neither art nor morality. With an excessive gullibility rather trying to the reader, Sidney allows others to maneuver him away from pure-hearted Jane into Clara's loveless arms. By the novel's end, the drudgery of supporting an embittered and scarred wife and her whole beggarly family forces the hero to renounce his art forever and even his creator's own favorite solace—the reading of good books (ch. xxxix, 374).

Another of Gissing's old idealized remedies—philanthropy—seems just as impotent as art within *The Nether World.* In the character of old Snowdon, philanthropy becomes a mere fanatic's illusion, a willingness to ruin a granddaughter's future for the sake of a muddle-headed dream. Jane Snowdon herself seems a slum-enfeebled version of Gissing's earlier female philanthropists. Although she has sweetness and altruism, her childhood victimization by the Peckovers has left her prone to hysterical fits. It has also stunted her book learning, her capacity for intellectual growth (ch. xv, 135–36). Easily manipulated by others and deprived of her rightful inheritance, she becomes reduced at the end to an impoverished philanthropist—one who can give sympathy but hardly any money to pathetic "Pennyloaf" Candy (ch. xl, 387–88).

Clara Hewett offers the book's most lurid example of how narrow circumstances thwart uncommon working people. Although she has acting talent, this proletarian woman can gain no chance to perform except by having sex with her theatrical sponsor (ch. ix,

88; ch. x, 94–96; ch. xxiii, 202–9). Clara refuses to imitate Sidney's judicious submission to working-class limits. She cannot accept his pessimistic farewell to high aspirations and art: "We are the lower orders; we are the working classes" (ch. vi, 58). As a result, she suffers far more acutely than any of the other characters, and her scarred face becomes a symbol of her blighted artistic ambitions.

In contrast to *Thyrza*'s tolerant portrayal of working-class amusements, Gissing returns in *The Nether World* to a disgusted condemnation of proletarian culture. In a key chapter entitled "Io Saturnalia!" or *hurrah for the Saturnalia*—a Roman festival that for once allowed slaves to do what they liked—Gissing's working people choose despicable entertainments: Crystal-Palace bread and circuses, barrelfuls of beer, and fights among the mob.[21] The chapter's heavy irony shifts, at one point, into an explicitly aesthetic condemnation of the masses: "Away to the west yonder the heavens are afire with sunset, but at that we do not care to look; never in our lives did we regard it. We know not what is meant by beauty or grandeur. Here under the glass roof stand white forms of undraped men and women—casts of antique statues—but we care as little for the glory of art as for that of nature . . ." (ch. xii, 110). In this, his final proletarian novel, his leave-taking of the genre, Gissing at last bitterly concedes that aesthetic idealism has no proper place in working-class fiction.

Chapter Three

Shabby Gentility and Upwards

In spite of Gissing's early attempts to describe working-class life, his finest novels deal with the middle class, although often with its bottom layers. His first efforts, however, to move completely away from proletarian subjects—*Isabel Clarendon* and *A Life's Morning*—reveal a sometimes immature fascination with elegant gentlemen and ladies, a fashionable world in which he always remained a somewhat uneasy intruder. Not until *The Emancipated* did Gissing avoid both the dinner jackets of his genteel novels and the overalls of his working-class ones—both the high and low extremes. Years later in his studies of Charles Dickens, Gissing noted a special Dickensian gift for describing the social stratum from which Dickens himself had sprung—the sparsely educated lower middle class.[1] Gissing, too, became the skillful chronicler of his own social stratum: a group of well-educated men and women without elegant ancestry; a group without rank derived from riches; a group, in fact, without distinguishing marks except for their own superior brains and their own sensitivity to their alienated state.

Isabel Clarendon

Although not wholly successful, *Isabel Clarendon* (written 1885; pub. 1886) marks a notable turning point in Gissing's artistic development—his first essentially nonproletarian novel. The only remnant of Gissing's concern with industrial and big-city squalor appears in two chapters that describe the hero's disgust at the vulgar avariciousness of his sister's landlady.[2] The hero, Bernard Kingcote, is educated and middle-class but without much money, and he falls in love with a fashionable widow who herself has sprung from a none-too-wealthy middle-class family. Throughout the book Gissing treats fashionable society with a mixture of admiration and faultfinding envy. Rather like an aristocrat, Kingcote himself avoids all gainful employment until the closing chapters, and he lives on dividends and interest. But unlike a true gentleman, the shabby-genteel hero cannot possibly afford a country estate. With barely enough income to support a humble existence, he rents a mere laborer's cottage on the heroine's vast property. There he leads a life that travesties aristocratic leisure: surrounded by fields of the wealthy, he labors not, neither does he spin, but he has to dwell in squalid lodgings.

As the novel opens, the city-dweller Kingcote impulsively rents a humble vacant cottage on Isabel Clarendon's rural estate. He has not yet seen this renowned country beauty, although he has met her ward, homely Ada Warren. And the hero does not know that the late Mr. Clarendon has allowed his widow only interim use of both his land and money until Ada, his illegitimate child, inherits almost everything by marrying or coming of age. Isabel has kept her temporary luxuries by submitting to her late husband's degrading command that she raise his bastard daughter. Ada herself remains wholly unaware of either her parentage or legacy, yet she resents her guardian's persistent unfriendliness. When the widow at last tells Ada the truth, the embittered ward becomes engaged to a cynical fortune hunter in order to hasten Isabel's loss of wealth. Deeply upset, the widow injures herself in a horseback-riding accident.

Although Kingcote has by now met the widow, he remains perversely miserable in his self-chosen solitude until her accident shocks him into revealing his adoration. He and the convalescing Isabel express mutual love and become engaged secretly, although this unconvincing scene fails to explain why a luxury-worshiping beauty should care in the least for a shabby-genteel loafer. In any case, money difficulties soon delay their marriage.

Returning to London, Kingcote unwillingly seeks work in order to support his impoverished and newly widowed sister and her boys. Isabel herself confesses to having incurred large debts, but when her ward's cynical fiancé postpones Ada's marriage, Isabel for the moment keeps the Clarendon wealth. As Ada in London becomes a professional writer, the still-unemployed Kingcote suffers hysterical jealousy over Isabel's fashionable life. Finally believing that she wishes to get rid of him, he unjustly suspects her of flirting with her rich male cousin. The frenzied hero notifies Isabel that he has broken their engagement, and then he falls gravely ill. When Ada nobly and quite unexpectedly renounces her inheritance so that Isabel may keep it, the now-secure widow gives Kingcote another chance to become her husband after all. Employed at last as a humble bookseller, Kingcote rejects her pity. Accordingly, she marries her friendly rich cousin, and the closing pages hint that the hero may eventually marry Ada.

Isabel Clarendon reveals Gissing's troubled ambivalence about the landed upper classes. At the novel's center lies the question of who shall inherit Isabel's mansion "Knightswell" and its large surrounding property. In the definitive study of nineteenth-century England's gentry and aristocracy, F. M. L. Thompson has shown that a big country estate formed the basic requirement for entrance into fashionable life. Land had an old connection with a traditional aristocratic symbol—a well-stocked stable of horses. In practical terms, a large estate permitted its owner to live without working, simply by drawing rent from his army of tenant farmers. Above all, England's laws of primogeniture passed big estates on from father to eldest son and thus helped maintain high family position down through the generations. And this permanent attachment to vast tracts of land gave patrician families social and also political dominance over surrounding country districts.[3] All of these points enter significantly into Gissing's first novel to concentrate upon landed country life.

The heroine herself, Isabel, holds a basically ambiguous position among the landed gentry. As the impoverished daughter of a prematurely dead rural solicitor (I, ch. ii, 28), she married Eustace Clarendon to gain social status. Yet although Clarendon owned a large estate and had also won a seat in Parliament, neither his land nor his money had aged long enough to make him a full-fledged gentleman. His stockbroker father had earned the Clarendon wealth but had failed to buy a country seat. Thus, Eustace Clarendon's purchase of Knightswell could not disguise his "*novus homo*" position (I, ch. iii, 56): his cash remained merely second-generation cash, and his land merely first-generation property. If we accept the old folk saying that "the third generation" of riches and rural estate "makes" the true "gentleman,"[4] Clarendon lacked true gentility. Behaving, in fact, like a low-born ruffian, he insulted and humiliated his wife. Symptomatically, Clarendon had no taste at all for the favorite pursuit of authentic landed gentlemen: riding to hounds; Isabel, by contrast, fox-hunted like a true-born lady. And when Isabel did not provide Clarendon with an heir, her husband took spiteful revenge by willing his estate to Ada—his bastard child by a low Cockney mother (I, ch. ii, 39–42; I, ch. vii, 133–35). If the ignoble purchaser of Knightswell lacked fashionable ancestors, he also failed to establish a Clarendon line of gentlemanly descendants.

When Kingcote becomes involved with the widowed Mrs. Clarendon, he both admires and dislikes her long-assumed role of landed gentlewoman. He appreciates her social graces but finds, to his disappointment, that this fox-hunting woman feels bored by great literary works and by other forms of high culture (I, ch. x, 206–7). In this respect, she resembles her unbookish cousin, the wealthy Robert Asquith (II, ch. ii, 58–59), whom she ultimately and appropriately marries. Although low-born himself, Kingcote does have a naturally aristocratic "intellect and temperament" (II, ch. v, 111), and he values the realm of landed country gentlemen for its "absence of . . . townish Radicalism" (I, ch. ix, 178). But he resents Isabel's love of fashionable parties among the unaesthetic rich (II, ch. iii, 83–84; II, ch. ix, 210–16). He finally breaks with her for preferring high society to his cultivated but shabby-genteel company. In depicting his hero's dilemma, Gissing expresses his own social yearnings and also his social grudges: a wish for the landed gentry's prosperous leisure, but also an envious presumption that he could use it more tastefully than they do. Because of the rather unconvincing relationship between the hero and the heroine, the book remains imperfect. Yet its often haunting descriptions of Kingcote's deep frustrations anticipate one of Gissing's finest novels—*Born in Exile* (1892)—a far more objective account of a natural aristocrat thwarted by a lowly social background.

A Life's Morning

Compared to *Isabel Clarendon, A Life's Morning* (written 1885; pub. 1888) seems clumsy in its conventional juxtaposition of fashionable life with shabby-genteel existence. Though the story of Emily Hood contains a strong middle section dealing with the heroine's lowly Yorkshire family, the beginning and end about Wilfrid Athel, gentleman, show Gissing at his snobbish worst. Yet George Orwell justly praised the middle chapters' account of the decline and fall of the heroine's luckless father.[5] In the E. P. Dutton edition of *A Life's Morning*, this episode takes up 134 pages out of 348—almost a novel in itself, and one well worth reading.[6]

At the beginning of the impressive section about the heroine's father, Emily Hood pays a visit to her hard-up Yorkshire parents but shrinks from telling them about her engagement to the son and heir of her wealthy employers in Surrey. Mr. and Mrs. Hood have a wretched married life: the thin-skinned father has failed in various businesses and has sunk to a paltry clerkship in a worsted mill, and the ex-schoolteacher mother has soured into a mere household drudge. Unexpectedly, however, Mr. Hood's boss, the mill owner Richard Dagworthy, falls in love with Emily and proposes to her. She, of course, rejects him because of her existing engagement to Wilfrid. But Dagworthy tries to coerce her into marrying him instead. He entices her father into stealing a ten-pound note and then secretly threatens Emily with her father's incrimination. When she still refuses to yield, the vengeful suitor dismisses Mr. Hood and denies him the reference that he must have for gaining other employment. Because of her painful dilemma, the heroine acts coldly toward the guilt-ridden Mr. Hood but does not tell him of the attempted blackmail. As a result, Hood slinks away and kills himself with poison. The most effective passages in this part of the story describe the father's pathetic temptation and his later doleful remorse. Yet even the scenes with Dagworthy achieve a touch of subtlety and avoid presenting him as an outright villain. The only weaknesses in the Hood-Dagworthy section derive from the narrator's constant idealization of the book-loving aesthetic heroine—a weakness that spills over from the rest of the novel.[7]

In contrast to the strong middle episode, the book's beginning and end seem as overly sentimental as anything else that Gissing ever wrote. With a false lyricism that mimics George Meredith, the narrator presents foppish Wilfrid Athel as a deep-souled and highly cultured gentleman who falls in love with deep-souled Emily, a less-than-beautiful governess heroine in the Charlotte Brontë mode. Because everyone has expected him to marry Beatrice Redwing, who has beauty, wealth, singing talent, and also religious fervor, his family opposes Wilfrid's unfashionable choice of his bride-to-be. At this point, the Hood-Dagworthy story interrupts the plot.

The novel's conclusion outdoes even the opening in sentimental idealism. Emily feels guilty at not having saved her father by submitting herself to Dagworthy. As a result, she renounces her engagement to the hero but refuses to tell him why. With the two lovers separated, the story skips ahead six and a half years to reveal Wilfrid as a not-very-convincing member of Parliament—a fashionable and golden-tongued orator. He engages himself to Beatrice, by now a professional singer, but happens to meet Emily in a park near Hampton Court and realizes that he still loves her. Not even pausing to break with his fiancée, he proposes again to his long-lost soulmate. When Emily eagerly accepts him, he hurries back to Beatrice to confess what he has done. She, in turn, behaves with exalted nobility and smoothes the way for him to marry the rival heroine and live happily ever after.

Within the book's weak beginning and ending, affected idealism and embarrassing snobbery reinforce each other. The hero's name itself, Athel, comes from an Old English word and means "nobility" or "noble ancestry." Gissing takes pains to stress that this third-generation heir of both land and money ranks as a bona fide gentleman. His grandfather earned the Athel wealth through grain—a thoroughly respectable commodity closely connected, in fact, with the landed aristocracy. Wilfrid's father avoided commerce altogether and became a world-traveling Egyptologist and a lover of country sports (ch. i, 4–5). Wilfrid himself goes from Oxford's Balliol College to a fashionable career in Parliament, although he plans to retire early, in gentlemanly leisure on his family's great estate (ch. i, 2; ch. xx, 272; ch. xxvi, 342–43).[8] On page after overwritten page, Gissing insists that Wilfrid combines the exalted virtues of both genteel squire and lover of the arts: "... He struck the note of good-breeding, he was unsurpassed in phrasing ... He was fast making of himself an artist in talk ..." (ch. xx, 275). But he had earlier yearned to "know every subtlest melody of verse in every tongue, enjoy with perfectly instructed taste every form that man has carved or painted" (ch. i, 15). These seriously intended invocations of both elitism and aestheticism cry out for corrective parody.

Some of the novel's cloying idealism affects even the strong middle part. Thus, the narrator stresses not only the heroine's ladylike grace, but also her love of literary classics that has made her "an artist in life" (ch. i, 11, 16; ch. iii, 34, 40). She practices a "religion of culture," of "beauty-worship" (ch. v, 69). Her petty-bourgeois parents feel "awe" at Emily's superior "nature so apart from" their "own" (ch. xi, 163). Even ruthless Dagworthy adores her "as the highest and holiest he knew" (ch. x, 151). But the narrator adds snobbishly that the mill owner's background in commerce allows him to mistreat this high aesthetic angel: "... His birth and breeding enabled him to accept meanness as almost a virtue in many of the relations and transactions of life. The trickery and low cunning of the mercantile world was in his blood . . ." (ch. x, 148). In this unintentional parody of aristocratic fastidiousness, the narrator almost equates a commercial career with villainy.

Gissing's friend Morley Roberts argued that the publisher's reader James Payn spoiled *A Life's Morning* by making the author revise his original ending—one in which Emily died.[9] Yet the heroine's death could hardly have saved the book from its idealized snobbery and sentimental aestheticism. Gissing, not Payn, weakened the Hood-Dagworthy story by embedding it within a silver-fork and silver-pen romance.

The Emancipated

The Emancipated (written 1889; pub. 1890) deserves an important place among Gissing's works, for it marks his first unqualified break with idealizing fiction, in contrast to *The Nether World*'s attempt to subvert idealism from within. One brief scene in *The Emancipated* makes specific fun of idealized novels: a vulgar young man named Bickerdike wins popular success with the "purity and idealism" of his "A Crown of Lilies"—a "romance" of "the noble and the pure."[10] *The Emancipated* has the identifying trait of Gissing's most mature fiction— a blend of ironic disillusionment and humane pity. But one distracting flaw has prevented the book from gaining the attention that it merits: in the course of three clumsy opening chapters, Gissing introduces fourteen important characters, each with a frigid little dossier. Yet after this inept and confusing beginning, Gissing unfolds his narrative with an admirable control—a control essentially ironic.[11]

The first chapters describe assorted English tourists in Naples: the widowed Miriam Baske, a narrow-minded Puritan; Cecily Doran, an enlightened young freethinker; and, as secondary figures, the pathetic Denyer sisters, pseudoemancipated and shabby-genteel Madeline, Barbara, and Zillah. When Miriam's scapegrace brother, freethinking Reuben Elgar, arrives and falls in love with Cecily, this young heiress's guardian, the painter Ross Mallard, tries to protect her from the unwise attachment but also to conceal his own love for her. Soon, however, Reuben and Cecily elope to England in a lyrical burst of euphoria.

Once in England, the newlyweds' joy gradually turns to mutual loathing. The hypocritic husband proclaims a double standard for his own and his wife's behavior. When a child is born, Reuben expresses little love for it, and Cecily herself refuses to become a full-time nursemaid. Although Reuben decides to produce a book on the history of English Puritanism, he loses his wife's remaining respect by never writing anything. Ironically enough, Cecily's very enlightenment—her freedom from religious dogma—only worsens matters between them, for it keeps her from judging his irresponsible acts as harshly as they deserve. Then Reuben engages in furtive sexual escapades, and Cecily's baby dies.

Meanwhile in Italy, Mallard pays court to a much-improved Miriam, who has outgrown most of her Puritanism but not her jealousy toward his ex-ward. In England, Cecily discovers Reuben's tawdry infidelities when a newspaper tells of his arrest in a brawl over a female music-hall vocalist. Soon this degraded man separates from Cecily. By contrast, Mallard finally marries Miriam, whom he has systematically trained into an artist's obedient helpmate. At the conclusion, Reuben is killed by the jealous husband of an unfaithful Parisian actress. In a touching final scene, Cecily learns of Reuben's sordid death, and she weeps for their lyrical past.

The Emancipated hinges upon an ethical question that preoccupied many late Victorians besides Gissing himself: can one discard religion and yet remain moral? The novel begins in 1878 (pt. I, ch. v, 75)—a time when this issue had aroused much discussion among English intellectuals. In 1877 an especially important debate on religion and morals—"A Modern Symposium"—had appeared in the prestigious *Nineteenth Century* magazine.[12] The debate was sponsored by the Metaphysical Society (1869–1880), whose membership included such British notables as Alfred, Lord Tennyson; James Anthony Froude; Sir Leslie Stephen; Sir James

Fitzjames Stephen; Thomas Henry Huxley; John Morley; and Frederic Harrison—the last two of whom later became, for a time, Gissing's friends and patrons.[13] Opinions within the printed "Symposium" cover a wide spectrum: the Dean of St. Paul's orthodox insistence upon the interdependence of morals and Christianity, Harrison's Comtist faith in the ethical power of a purely human worship, and Huxley's belief that morals can survive the death of religion. In words with a special relevance to *The Emancipated*, Huxley argues that morality stands closer to aesthetics than to any formal creed: "I see no reason for doubting that the beauty of holiness and the ugliness of sin are, to a great many minds, no mere metaphors, but feelings as real and as intense as those with which the beauty or ugliness of form or colour fills the artist mind, and that they are as independent of intellectual beliefs, and even of education, as are all the true aesthetic powers and impulses."[14] *The Emancipated*, in fact, goes a step beyond Huxley's analogy and connects ethics specifically with culture and aesthetics, very much in the manner of Matthew Arnold's *Culture and Anarchy* (1869). Also like Arnold, however, Gissing insists that authentic artists must have high ethical values—a sympathy and concern for mankind's joys and sorrows.

Within the private consciences of five major figures, Gissing investigates the various effects of losing one's faith or having none to lose. Thus, Miriam Baske's gradual enlightenment shows that some persons can abandon religious belief and yet become more sensitive than ever before in both moral judgment and conduct. She begins as a joyless Dissenter—an exponent of that same nineteenth-century Puritanism scorned by Arnold for its unaesthetic "disputes, tea-meetings, openings of chapels, sermons."[15] She ends by substituting high artistic culture for chapelgoing militancy and by learning to control her intolerance, jealousy, and pride. For Miriam, however, religion's decline leads to eventual wisdom only because she benefits from an out-of-school training in the true Gissing curriculum: literature, foreign languages, painting, and classical history. At one point, she even submits to the painter-hero's oral examination on how to judge great art (pt. II, ch. vii,

332). Indeed, the only weakness in Gissing's portrayal of his heroine's "emancipation" comes from creeping male chauvinism. In one somewhat embarrassing passage, for example, the narrator extols "the happiness" open to Miriam through submitting to "a [man] stronger than herself," a wise aesthetic man like the hero (pt. II, ch. viii, 341).

Mallard exemplifies the artist as moral human being. He has actually received an early indoctrination in ethics as well as in art. If his patron, Mr. Doran, financed the young man's lessons in painting, Doran also trained the lad in "accepted moral" values (pt. I, ch. v, 80–81). And Mallard dutifully lives by those values. His code requires that he go on creating in spite of any emotional strains or thwarted romantic desires. Thus, when beautiful Cecily elopes with Reuben, Mallard conquers his jealousy and his sexual frustration, and, with stoical self-control, paints fine landscapes. Later, he feels scorn for Reuben, the would-be writer who never does write but merely wastes his time.

Although Reuben has cast off his Puritan background and has embraced high culture, he lacks the discipline to produce his own art or even to behave as a decent human being. His hypocritical abuse of his admirable wife coincides, step by step, with his total inability to stick to his writing. His literary and domestic inadequacies spring from one source: a wholly selfish hedonism. Although he offers the excuse that the laws of the physical universe have predetermined his baseness and failure (pt. I, ch. vi, 108, 115; pt. II, ch. x, 365–66), his self-justification seems a materialistic parody of the chapelgoing faith that he himself has rejected: the belief that grace can come from God alone and not from man's own merits.

Cecily stands as Gissing's most convincingly appealing heroine before *New Grub Street.* Having shed her Puritan doctrines and learned a love of art, she belongs with the truly "emancipated" few and not the pseudo-"emancipated" many. At first she cannot tell a dedicated artist from a mere intemperate trifler, for she marries Elgar instead of Mallard. She does see through the pretensions of the fake artist Marsh, who lacks talent or even minimal taste.

Reuben himself has taste but cannot do anything with it. Cecily soon understands her error and later endures her deeply unhappy marriage with both dignity and strength. Her mistake, in fact, came from youthful inexperience rather than from any inherent moral flaw. At the beginning, her innocence allowed her to think that "the artist is born a prince among men" and need not obey "the rules by which common people" live (pt. I, ch. ii, 28). By the end, she has learned that even the greatest artists must adhere to the common decencies.

In contrast to brave Cecily stands pathetic Madeline Denyer. Through Madeline's appalling miseries, Gissing illustrates the forlornness of a nonmoral aestheticism faced with the ills of flesh. She claims to believe in art yet falls in love with Marsh, an atrociously bad painter. When an accident leaves Madeline a hopeless paraplegic, Marsh abandons her entirely and she loses her interest in art. With no resources left, she lies on her sickbed and wallows in lugubrious self-pity. As death approaches, she expresses an anguished wish to believe in a comforting afterlife, but Madeline confesses her bewildered uncertainty about any truths at all (pt. II, ch. xiii, 404). She might better have followed the example of the family spinster Zillah; this plain, dull woman has abandoned all pretense of high artistic taste in favor of simple piety (pt. II, ch. xiii, 401). With a tolerance that Gissing had often lacked before, *The Emancipated* displays a preference for morality—even a religious morality—over an aestheticism stripped of ethical values.

Chapter Four

Two Major Achievements: *New Grub Street* and *Born in Exile*

New Grub Street

New Grub Street (1891) stands as Gissing's masterpiece and also one of the finest novels of the late-Victorian era. Part of its strength comes from his finally having restricted all his major characters in a novel to an occupation that he knew firsthand—the writer's profession. Every important male character writes for a living, as do many of the important females, and the other major women marry writers. As a result, *New Grub Street* avoids a common weakness of the novelist's lesser fiction: fabricated vocations stuck unconvincingly onto the characters' lives. In this most impressive example of Gissing's realism, work and domestic life form a seamless whole.

New Grub Street also draws strength from its ironic yet sympathetic exposure of illusory idealism—an idealism that fails to recognize that "everything is relative."[1] Although Reardon, for example, resents his wife's failure to act like an "ideal" helpmate (ch. ix, 133), he ultimately admits that only a person with "shallow idealism" could blame either her or him for the chilling effects of poverty (ch. xvii, 236). Then, too, his friend Harold Biffen dismisses Reardon's fantasy of a perfect marriage with a working-class wife as the dream of "a shameless idealist" (ch. xxvii, 392). Later Biffen censures Reardon's "obstinate idealism" in remaining apart from Amy after she has inherited enough wealth to make them both comfortable (ch. xxxi, 471). Marian Yule falls in love with all-too-"human" Jasper Milvain simply because "ideal personages do not descend to girls who have to labour at the British Museum" (ch. xiv, 197–98). The romantically susceptible literary man, Whelpdale, endures four jiltings by successive fiancées—the last a young woman who fulfills his absolute "ideal" (ch. xvi, 228, 231). Believing in no "absolute ideals," Reardon concedes the absurdity of his moral distaste for writing potboilers (ch. iv, 53). And Milvain openly confesses that his own triumphs have sprung from a total lack of ideals: "It is men of my kind who succeed; the conscientious, and those who really have a high ideal, either perish or struggle on in neglect" (ch. xxxvi, 539).

Almost every page of the novel undercuts two aspects of life idealized in Gissing's earlier fiction: sexual love and art. A single tough-minded principle runs through *New Grub Street*: in a society that values only money, neither love nor art can flourish without sufficient cash. This one simple precept shapes the narrative pattern of intricate parallels, foreshadowings, repetitions, and disillusioned ironies. In chapter i, Jasper Milvain, a cynical young journalist, expounds to his mother and sisters the book's central themes as he compares his own practical aims with Edwin Reardon's high-minded imprudence. Milvain associates his unwise friend with a man who, according to the newspaper, faces hanging in London at that very instant. In Milvain's view, Reardon will cause his own eventual downfall by two fundamental blunders; he writes novels for the sake of art rather than for the market, and he has picked a wife with elegant tastes but virtually no dowry. A point needs underlining here: Jasper is no villain. With rather likable humor, he accepts the intractable realities that shape the novel's world. He foretells the narrative future with complete accuracy. Reardon *will* undo himself by not writing for the market. His wife *will* resent their poverty. And Milvain himself *will* succeed by writing for "the upper middle-class of" the reading public's "intellect" and by marrying a wealthy woman (ch. i, 10).

In contrast to a genuine villain, Jasper likes and even respects the novel's most upright characters. In fact, as the story proceeds, he becomes deflected from his smoothly cynical course by the attractiveness of Marian Yule, who does literary slave work for her embittered old father, the hack writer Alfred Yule. Jasper's response to this woman with neither wealth nor conventional beauty reveals his sexual taste for human fineness: Marian is, in fact, the book's most admirable person, with warmth, sensitivity, intelligence, and gentle concern for others, but also moral toughness in adversity.[2] Yet Jasper's very awareness of her excellence serves to underscore Gissing's basic point: in a life of material want, even splendid human qualities wither. In context, Jasper's conviction that poverty brings debasement represents more than a mere personal quirk. Alfred Yule's good-natured working-class wife says that "poverty will make the best people bad" (ch. vii, 90). Reardon and his wife both say so (ch. xv, 211–12). Even Marian eventually confesses that money enables "one to live a better and fuller life" (ch. xxx, 446). And Reardon's friend, Harold Biffen, a struggling but unmarried novelist, provides a detailed theory of just how poverty degrades human lives: "ignobly decent" people—those with good intentions but insufficient money—remain "at the mercy of paltry circumstance" in both love and work (ch. x, 150–52).

The collapse of Reardon's marriage to genteel Amy exemplifies Biffen's theory about the "ignobly decent." The very first page on which the Reardons appear describes the wife's satisfaction with their presentable flat across from Regent's Park—a home that they can barely afford on Edwin's uncertain income from fiction. Later their quarrels center around this residential emblem of middle-class propriety. Amy bristles at her husband's suggestion that they give up the place for cheaper lodgings. She agrees to vacate only if Edwin leaves for a respectable country vacation, during which he can pursue his writing, while the baby and she move to her mother's dainty home. But her face-saving plans collapse when he cannot sell the novel that would have paid for everything. Desperately, he accepts a post as a mere hospital clerk (his job in early bachelor days) and insists that they move to a low-rent London district. Reardon complains that he can no longer write well because of money pressures from living above their means. But Amy opposes his taking an undignified clerkship, and she also refuses to move to cheaper rooms. As a result of their disagreement on these "ignobly decent" points, she separates from her husband.

"Ignobly decent" details also spoil their attempt to get back together and ultimately, in fact, cause Edwin's death. Because of insults from Amy's family, he endures squalor and worn-out clothes in order to send her half his income. As a result, when he finally gets an adequate job offer—a secretaryship at a Croydon boys' school—and visits Amy to ask her to rejoin him, she feels disgust and shame at his unkempt appearance, and he feels disgust at her disgust. Their reconciliation founders on such rubbishy little things as the perspiration stain around his hatband. Not even Amy's subsequent legacy of £10,000 from an uncle can heal the marital rift, mainly because both the husband and the wife still feel resentment over the mutual bitterness caused by Edwin's shabby clothing. And a final disastrous consequence results from their ignoble meeting. Because Reardon's overcoat has become too threadbare for even his humbled pride, he walks coatless to see Amy and so catches cold. Throughout their later estrangement, his cold gets steadily worse. When she finally wires him to come to her in Brighton because their child had caught diphtheria, Edwin travels to Amy through a snowy night in spite of his own alarming lung congestion. Although the husband and wife at last make up, their reunion ends in calamity: first the child dies and then Edwin himself expires. The trivial chain of events that began with his shabby clothing destroys the couple's chance to retrieve their lost happiness.

Running parallel to the Amy-Edwin marriage, Jasper's half-unwilling courtship of Marian derives sardonic bite from contrasts with the Reardons' engagement. In order to avoid "ignobly decent" wedlock and a moneyless career as a writer, Jasper shrinks from Marian although he often passes her in the British Museum Reading Room. But, overcome at last by her attractiveness, he condescends to take her home through a choking London fog—a fog she associates with her dull literary labors. When he cautiously asks her to befriend his two sisters, who have moved to the city to become professional writers, a paltry new difficulty arises. Alfred Yule resents Marian's friendliness with Jasper, partly because the young man writes for an editor whom Alfred despises. In addition, however, Alfred wishes his daughter to remain his perpetual literary slave. Though Marian defies her father, her reluctant lover warns her of his need to marry someone with money rather than settle for Marian's cashless attractions.

Not even Marian's unexpected legacy from an uncle of hers and Amy's can dispel the financial problems involved in courtship, for Gissing avoids treating Grub Street inheritances as simple miraculous deliverances. Although Marian will get £5,000, Jasper thinks this inadequate for smoothing his literary path, and he also feels annoyed that Marian's cousin Amy will get exactly double this amount. Moreover, Marian's father wants to use her prospective cash for starting his very own magazine. But she resists his scheme for two cogent reasons: he lacks the wisdom for success, and she herself needs money to lure Jasper into marriage. With what Jasper regards as sheer "magnanimity" (ch. xxiv: "Jasper's Magnanimity"), he at last proposes to Marian, in spite of his disappointment at her rather small legacy. She accepts him, and they await the expected sum of cash, but instead only misfortune arrives. Her embittered father learns that he is going blind—the worst possible illness for a writer. And the firm that owes Marian her inheritance collapses into bankruptcy. Jasper, of course, insists on delaying their planned marriage until they can better afford it. If his moral twistings provide subacid comedy, they also fit the story's basic assumptions about the unwiseness of wedlock on small amounts of money. When Marian at last receives only £1,500 of the original bequest, she admits that she must use it to help her afflicted father. As a result, Jasper proposes to an unattractive heiress without even bothering to break first with Marian, but the heiress unexpectedly rejects him. Although he lacks the nerve to renounce his engagement, he at last humiliates Marian into renouncing it herself.

To help Marian support her ill-fated parents, Alfred Yule's friends find her a place as a small-town librarian—an ironic final haven for a woman who loathed the British Museum Reading Room. As the story closes, Milvain marries the now-widowed Amy and her £10,000. Significantly, however, he feels genuine love for his wife. He also behaves generously toward struggling fellow writers once he himself has risen to an influential editorship. In Jasper Milvain's case, money does smooth the way for both love and literary triumph.

The theme of money's importance to both literary creation and marriage reverberates through the lives of even those characters who play minor roles in the story. Thus, Marian's pathetic mother illustrates an alternate choice for impoverished writers: instead of marrying an elegant wife, settle for a working-class one. But although this humble woman displays far more patience and gentleness toward grumpy Mr. Yule than Amy does toward Reardon, Yule complains constantly of his wife's proletarian speech, her abysmal ignorance, and her unpolished efforts to act as a hostess for his literary friends. Harold Biffen provides still another example of what happens through lack of money. If his novel, "Mr. Bailey, Grocer," shows how poverty reduces good human beings to mere ignoble decency (ch. xvi, 223), his own actual life dramatizes the point. As a result of his wretched lodgings, he nearly loses his manuscript in a fire caused by a grimy, drunken neighbor. This struggling writer, in fact, retains his courage amid squalid surroundings only so long as he stays aloof from all erotic entanglements. In the end he makes the same mistake that Reardon had made: Biffen becomes infatuated with the now-widowed Amy. But realizing the hopelessness of his unrequited love, he kills himself with a poison that he had carefully researched at the British Museum Reading Room. Like half a dozen still lesser characters, Biffen demonstrates the ultimate futility of idealism in either love or art.

The novel emphasizes one basic paradox in the lives of late-Victorian writers: they work at a slow and ancient handicraft amid rapidly changing communication technology. Milvain notes that old Grub Street lacked telegraphy (ch. i, 5). He also identifies his own journalistic zeal with a speeding railroad train ("it en-spirits me"—ch. iii, 31)—a prime example of nineteenth-century mechanized efficiency. Yet although machines can speed up and expand the distribution of writing, Gissing's authors must still create in the ancient laborious way, word by word, sentence by sentence, page by page, with old-fashioned pen and paper. Books, in particular, take a long time to write, far longer than most other craft-produced goods. The conscientious novelist Reardon needs a full seven months to achieve his very best work (ch. xv, 214). The equally scrupulous Biffen takes just as long with his "Mr. Bailey, Grocer": "He worked very slowly. . . . Each sentence was as good as he could make it, harmonious to the ear, with words of precious meaning skillfully set. Before sitting down to a chapter he planned it minutely in his mind; then he wrote a rough draft of it; then he elaborated the thing phrase by phrase" (ch. xxxi, 456). But when the need for money compels Reardon to hurry, he starts a book without adequate planning, keeps changing subjects, and commits "intolerable faults" of accidental rhyme and clumsy rhythm (ch. ix, 128–30). He contrasts his botched prose with the great poetry of *The Odyssey*: "*that* was not written at so many pages a day, with a workhouse clock clanging its admonition at the poet's ear" (ch. ix, 131).

The struggle against time, the conflict between quality and speed, dominates the lives of *New Grub Street*'s writers. Marian Yule feels so oppressed by these occupational tensions that she ironically envisions a "Literary Machine," a mechanical author for adapting, reducing, and blending "old books" into marketable new ones (ch. viii, 111–12). Jasper, on the other hand, aims at human writing efficiency, although on a bad day he produces only a page (ch. xxii, 322–23). But during one especially productive spurt, he dashes off a book review, a regular feature article, half of a short essay, and part of a longer piece in a mere thirteen hours and fifteen minutes (ch. xiv, 190–91). Jasper, of course, concentrates on journalism, but he insists that, if he had the talent, he would grind out novels with the same commercial efficiency (ch. i, 10). Yet his sister's question about "the value" of his high-speed writing raises a central issue of *New Grub Street.* When Jasper replies that his day's worth of work will bring in "ten to twelve guineas," she explains that she meant its "literary value," and the amused journalist revises his estimate: "equal to that of the contents of a mouldy nut" (ch. xiv, 191).

Like humble nineteenth-century craftsmen such as carpenters, shoemakers, or tailors, Gissing's writers gain their living by selling what they make. And the quicker they make their works of prose, the more they will earn for each day of labor. But in their writing, Reardon and Biffen aim at a transcendental value beyond time and without a cash equivalent—a value called art. In contrast with, say, a maker of custom chairs who can raise his price for his painstaking work, Gissing's serious literary men get paid at the same rate as any slapdash journalist. In fact, they get paid rather less, because they strive for other effects than the current market demands. Apart from the isolation of these scrupulous writers amid capitalism's technological progress, they exemplify the survival of an almost religious reverence toward the written word—a reverence that harks back at least a thousand years to the age of theological faith. Although Reardon and Biffen do not believe in God, they worship great writing as though it contains the spirit of the Divine.

In spite of Reardon's and Biffen's veneration for the word, they experience inner conflict because they partially share their era's material values. Reardon feels obsessed by money's beneficent power, and even the tougher Biffen can write cadenced prose only about people who suffer from lack of cash and of ordinary middle-class comforts. "You," he tells Reardon, "are repelled by what has injured you; I am attracted by it" (ch. x, 151). In addition, neither writer achieves the unworldly goal of creating great art: at best, their careful work stands slightly above average. As a result, one can sympathize with Jasper's ironic complaint about these unsuccessful literary artists: "What the devil . . . is there in typography to make everything it deals with sacred?" (ch. i, 10). It seems a measure of Gissing's advance in objectivity that *New Grub Street* does not allow us to dismiss Jasper's question as mere shallow cynicism. Indeed, the question reverberates throughout the entire book.[3]

In the following key passage, note the tough-minded eloquence, the psychological conviction, but also the sardonic humor of Marian Yule's despairing vision of the British Museum Reading Room, where she slaves at tasks assigned by her father:

> The fog drew thicker; she looked up at the windows beneath the dome and saw that they were a dusky yellow. Then her eye discerned an official walking along the upper gallery, and in pursuance of her grotesquė humour, her mocking misery, she likened him to a black, lost soul, doomed to wander in an eternity of vain research along endless shelves. Or again, the readers who sat here at these radiating lines of desks, what were they but hapless flies caught in a huge web, its nucleus the great circle of the Catalogue? Darker, darker. From the towering wall of volumes seemed to emanate visible motes, intensifying the obscurity; in a moment the book-lined circumference of the room would be but a featureless prison-limit. (ch. viii, 112)

The ancient association of books and religion affects the entire paragraph, yet Marian's depression gives an ironic hue to ostensibly Christian imagery. The Reading Room's literary drudges resemble scribal monks, like those who produced the theological library described in Arnold's "Stanzas from the Grande Chartreuse" (1855):

> The library, where tract and tome
> Not to feed priestly pride are there,
> To hymn the conquering march of Rome,
> Nor yet to amuse, as ours are!
> They paint of souls the inner strife,
> Their drops of blood, their death in life.[4]

But in far more famous words from the same poem, Gissing's literary hacks stand condemned to wander "between two worlds, one dead, / The other powerless to be born."[5] These toilers among books have lost the divine afflatus yet cannot adjust to the mechanized ways of modern industrial factories. The Reading Room itself, however, serves as an old-fashioned factory for recycling printed words.

In Marian's caustic vision of the British Museum Reading Room, traditional religious symbols become merely bitter images for conveying literary futility. The fog that snuffs out sunlight suggests infernal as well as mental darkness. Marian compares the upper gallery's walker to a damned soul in Hell condemned forever to a fruitless reference hunt along infinite rows of books. This "black, lost" researcher may have literal difficulty in tracking down a scholarly citation, but, figuratively, he has lost the light of God. As Marian gazes at other readers extending along the spokes of the library's vast circle, she perceives these drudges in terms of Satanic torment: "flies" who have blundered into a spider web merely to be devoured. The Catalogue stands at the room's literal center but also functions like a predator: ensconced in the middle of its web, the spiderlike Catalogue deludes the swarm of readers with vain reference clues. The gloom deepens even more infernally, as "visible motes," or dark specks, appear to emerge from the Reading Room's many "volumes"; God's written word has become debased into an instrument of mental blindness. The final image of the Library as a circular prison reflects an historical and architectural oddity. Jeremy Bentham's 1790s design of a model penitentiary called the "panopticon"—"a circular . . . structure" with the guards' observation "rotunda" at the center—[6] influenced the design of the British Museum Reading Room. Thus, Marian's initial vision of eternal damnation shrinks to a mere jail: a secular punishment imposed by society upon living men and women. In contrast with Gissing's idealizing novels, *New Grub Street* holds nothing sacred, not even the art of literature. Because of its hard-headed realism and its self-mocking balance, the work achieves a remarkable advance over Gissing's earlier books.

Born in Exile

Born in Exile (1892) contains Gissing's finest work as a psychological realist—a portrayer of a subtle mind's complex interaction with a convincing social milieu. The book centers around Godwin Peak, a brilliant yet self-tormenting agnostic from the lower middle classes who adopts the respectable camouflage of a candidate for the clergy because he aims at marrying a gentlewoman. The remarkable portrait of this troubled hero makes the novel one of Gissing's major achievements. The only slight flaw comes from perfunctory minor characters, such as Christian Moxey and Malkin, who inhabit weak little subplots. These seem designed to pad out the book to the three-volume length still expected by many late-Victorian publishers.[7] The secondary elements seem especially disappointing compared with the Yules and Biffens of *New Grub Street*—a novel far more deft than *Born in Exile* at using many characters in counterpoint to a single overriding theme. Indeed, *Born in Exile*'s central motif—the fragile imbalance of human consciousness when it tries to break away from social conventionality—appears ill-suited to the old-fashioned multiplotted structure.[8] Luckily, however, the Christian Moxey and Malkin episodes take up little space: they represent a small distraction in a generally masterful book.

In *Born in Exile* Gissing solves a basic problem of literary realism: how to imitate life's usually trivial flow and at the same time achieve coherent narrative form. In the past he had relied upon traditional plot devices, such as the sexual rivalry of two contrasting heroines or salvation by sudden inheritance. In Peak's story, however, the external events seem so basically unimportant that they avoid the appearance of contrivance. Yet meaning and form emerge from Peak's frantic effort to turn a commonplace meeting with former wealthy acquaintances into the social chance of a lifetime. Trifling occurrences derive both depth and point from Peak's grandiose aspirations and also his sense of shame.

The novel begins with a ceremony of academic awards at provincial Whitelaw College: Godwin Peak takes first prize in Logic and Moral Philosophy. His triumph in this discipline sends ironic reverberations throughout the entire story, which hinges upon his guilt-ridden attempt to perpetuate an intellectual fraud. The prize does not satisfy Peak, for he finishes only second in most of his other subjects. He also feels embarrassment as a poor scholarship boy when he meets the well-bred Warricombes, whose son has tied Peak for first prize in Geology (Geology here exemplifies the assault of nineteenth-century science upon religious orthodoxy). Most unexpectedly of all, he feels barely repressed fury at the plan of Andrew Peak, a bumptious Cockney uncle, to capitalize on the nephew's college career by opening "Peak's" café just across fom the campus.[9] The hero's response seems far out of proportion to the ridiculous annoyance, but he thinks himself one of nature's aristocrats, born through ill fate into a humble family—hence the title *Born in Exile.* When Andrew persists in his eating-place scheme, Peak leaves Whitelaw abruptly and instead decides to study industrial chemistry at the Royal School of Mines. He rationalizes his academic retreat as a way of avoiding further humiliation from additional second prizes.

Next the narrative skips ten years of the hero's "gnawing discontent, intervals of furious revolt, periods of black despair" (pt. II, ch. ii, 138). Although he earns good wages at a Rotherhithe chemical factory, lives in comfortable rooms, and mingles with Bohemian intellectuals, he yearns for acceptance by country gentlefolk, and he dreams of "marrying a lady" (pt. II, ch. ii, 151). Again events hinge upon the hero's disdain for his external circumstances. During a summer's vacation Peak visits Exeter, enters its famous cathedral, and happens to see Sidwell Warricombe, along with other members of that same elegant family whom he had known at Whitelaw. This chance meeting takes an undramatic form, for the hero doubts that the people are really Warricombes, and they ignore him completely. Yet he clutches at the occasion as a means to his visionary goal of a genteel marriage. He consults a local directory, questions his hotel landlord, and walks several miles to see the Warricombe estate. On Sunday he attends morning cathedral service and again glimpses Sidwell, the beautiful eldest daughter, at whom he stares like a snobbish voyeur. He lingers at Exeter and finally is noticed by his old fellow student, Buckland Warricombe. Throughout the whole episode Gissing provides a subtle psychological complication: the scheming Peak cannot admit to himself that he has all but arranged this "accidental" encounter. He carries out his conspiratorial plans with his consciousness averted from his aims.

A luncheon invitation finally gets the hero inside the Warricombe mansion, but at mealtime he arouses Buckland's suspicions by praising yesterday's sermon, although this former schoolmate had known Peak at college as bitterly antireligious. When he meets the crisis brilliantly with an improvised analysis of the minister's discourse, the pleased reactions of both Sidwell and of old Mr. Warricombe tempt the hero into further dissimulation. Soon he announces his resolve to study for the Anglican clergy. He feels immediate shame at what he has done but attempts to regard his hypocrisy as a kind of psychic jack-in-the-box sprung, without his consent, from the depths of his unconscious. Once again, an eruption from Peak's complex mind has added a strange intensity to an outwardly minor event.

Peak himself also sets in motion the chain of petty occurrences that ultimately undoes him. He receives proofs of an article that he had written earlier attacking church apologetics. Out of author's pride, he returns it for publication, though he leaves the piece unsigned in an effort to protect his continuing religious masquerade. His decision to publish this antichurch diatribe seems particularly risky in view of Buckland's growing suspicions about Peak's orthodox faith. Indeed, the hero's awareness of the ongoing danger keeps him in constant tension.

In spite of all the risks, Peak takes lodgings in Exeter, hides from his London Bohemian friends, and pursues his campaign of attaching himself to the Warricombes. He studies what he considers silly biblical commentaries to ingratiate himself with pious Mr. Warricombe, though the hero's performance as defender of the faith makes him sometimes doubt his very identity. Then a complicated change within Peak's mind again causes events to swerve. Instead of regarding Sidwell as merely a means to gentility, he now decides that he loves her for herself alone. Though shame almost persuades him to abandon his fraud, he hints to her of his love, and her encouraging reply makes him resolve on "Sidwell or death" (pt. III, ch. v, 296).

The novel's subtle conclusion juxtaposes the hero's authentic conversion to love with the sudden exposure of his sham religious conversion. Buckland at last encounters Peak's Bohemian friends, and one of them reveals the hero's authorship of the antireligious essay. Meanwhile Peak proposes to Sidwell, and she all but accepts him, but Buckland quickly unmasks her newly professed suitor as a theological fraud. Yet Peak has so influenced this pious young woman that she now discards her own religious faith and even permits her deeply disgraced lover to hope that she might marry him eventually. He feels exasperated, in fact, at the ironic possibility that he might have won Sidwell without the slightest deception. Then a freethinking woman friend of Peak's, who had helped to expose him out of jealousy, dies in an accident and leaves him her wealth. Freed from financial worries, he proposes again to Sidwell, yet she shrinks from breaking with her family and social class, and thus turns him down after all. Peak tries to forget her by traveling alone on the Continent, but he catches malaria in Naples, flees to Vienna, and dies in a transients' hotel. If Peak has always considered himself a man "born in exile" (pt. I, ch. v, 112), now he has died "in exile" (pt. VII, ch. iii, 547). But his alienation goes beyond mere geography or even humble origins, for this brilliant man has cut himself off from all social groupings, whether high or low, by his own self-condemning pride.

Compared with Gissing's masterful account of how Peak shapes his own ironic destiny, the subplots seem unnecessary and clumsy. For instance, a character named Malkin wanders around the world on unlimited supplies of money and rattles off supposedly comic speeches filled with "deuce," "confound it," and "whew" (pt. II, ch. i, 119). He concocts a plan of training his wife-to-be from puberty to adulthood, almost gets trapped instead into marrying the frumpish mother, but at last gains his custom-made and wholly enlightened bride. Another subplot character, the languid Christian Moxey, rebuffs the affections of his plain but admirable cousin in order to remain platonically faithful to a frivolous married woman. When her husband at last dies and she spurns the devoted Moxey, he marries the cousin after all. These farcical digressions remind one of the Emerson subplot in *Thyrza*, which served as a parody of the main plot's sentimentalism,[10] but the sardonic account of Peak's deceitful courtship hardly calls for parody. Those secondary characters who do fit *Born in Exile*'s dry-eyed toughness tend to stand apart from the subplots: Sidwell's witty and beautiful friend, Sylvia Moorhouse—a lady too emancipated for the arrogant tastes of the hero; and Bruno Chilvers—a mannered and effeminate Broad-Churchman, whose fatuous hodgepodge of science and theology embarrasses Peak by its eerie resemblance to his own religious fraud.

Even the novel's social details—above all, the gracious manners of the wealthy middle-class Warricombes—receive their distinctive quality from the way that Peak sees them. The Warricombes' lifestyle appeals to him as the answer to his frustrated needs. His highly subjective impression of these Devonshire gentry conveys the feeling of verisimilitude mainly because Peak himself convinces us as a character. He seems one of the earliest fictional portrayals of an English social phenomenon that became commonplace only by the mid-twentieth century: the scholarship boy cut off from his own humble origins.[11]

Richard Hoggart has provided a detailed account of twentieth-century scholarship boys in England, and his analysis of this sociological type corresponds quite closely to *Born in Exile*'s hero, although it does not, of course, match the intense evocation of Peak's lonely arrogance. In essence, Hoggart sees the scholarly son of the poor as lost between two worlds: he can no longer respect his own family's culture, but neither can he win the respect that he desires from cultivated middle-class people. His bookish learning and his test-taking skills have carried him into a social void. He resents the cheap clothing, the inelegant speech, and the unrefined manners of his parents, but he still feels uneasy about his own clothes, pronunciation, and manners. He tends to blame his lack of poise upon the group that bore him instead of blaming himself and his own rootlessness. Among well-to-do people, he remains self-conscious and tense. He usually leads a gloomy and isolated life and finds it hard to make friends "even with others in his condition." Worst of all, he feels anguished at "the discrepancy between his lofty pretensions and his lowly acts."[12] Hoggart's description fits Godwin Peak well, except for the minor divergence that Peak's unpretentious mother does have country relations in at least "decent circumstances" (pt. I, ch. ii, 31–32). Of a slightly higher status than a lower-class scholarship boy, Peak can more readily identify with the values of the landed rich: "men and women who represented the best in English society" (pt. II, ch. iii, 174).

Each social grace that Peak sees in the Warricombes reverses one of his own social failings. He admires Sidwell's cool "self-possession" but suffers from self-consciousness (pt. II, ch. iii, 166). Stiff and nervous himself, he esteems the Warricombes for their civilized tranquility (pt. II, ch. iv, 185). He feels attracted by Sidwell's "sweetness" but remains an essentially harsh and resentful man (pt. II, ch. iv, 184). He cherishes Sidwell's privileged "grace" but considers himself absolutely graceless (pt. III, ch. iv, 265). Above all, he regards these opposites of his own social faults as "qualities which characterise a class" (pt. III, ch. ii, 236).[13] In Gissing's earlier novels he frequently idealized the splendors of wealthy gentlefolk. The Warricombes' graces, however, derive much of their splendor from Peak's own brain. Because he needs to fill his own social hollowness, he magnifies the virtues of this rich provincial family out of all proportion. And, ironically, he gains Sidwell's eventual confidence by the reverse side of his unrestrained esteem for well-bred landed gentry: his hatred of his own background. By criticising the flaws of the petty bourgeoisie, he arouses the deepest sympathies of this woman with an "aristocratic temperament" (pt. III, ch. v, 291–92).

After extolling the virtues of English gentlefolk for several hundred pages, Peak suffers rejection by Sidwell, that poised and gracious gentlewoman. Immediately afterwards, he announces a revised social "ideal": intellectual cosmopolitans in Paris, Rome, and throughout the European continent (pt. VII, ch. i, 521). But he dies before he can find an enlightened female citizen of the world who feels inclined to have him. The reader pities Godwin Peak's frustrations yet never forgets the role of this highly intelligent man in creating his own troubles. Gissing depicts his self-deceiving hero with considerable compassion yet also without the slightest sentimentality.

Born in Exile achieves particular impressiveness in those passages that analyze the hero's self-deception. The following remarkable description of Godwin Peak's shame occurs right after he has announced his intention of studying for the clergy:

> What had happened seemed to him incredible; it was as though he revived a mad dream, of ludicrous coherence. Since his display of rhetoric at luncheon all was downright somnambulism. What fatal power had subdued him? What extraordinary influence had guided his tongue, constrained his features? His conscious self had had no part in all this comedy; now for the first time was he taking count of the character he had played. . . .
>
> Yet such possiblity had not been unforeseen. At the times of his profound gloom, when solitude and desire crushed his spirit, he had wished that fate would afford him such an opportunity of knavish success. His imagination had played with the idea that a man like himself might well be driven to this expedient, and might even use it with life-long result. . . .
>
> . . . A cowardly instinct, this; having once acted upon it gave to his whole life a taint of craven meanness. Mere bluster, all his talk of mental dignity and uncompromising scorn of superstitions. A weak and idle man, whose best years were already wasted!
>
> He gazed deliberately at himself in the glass, at his red eyelids and unsightly lips. Darkness was best; perhaps he might forget his shame for an hour or two ere the dawn renewed it. He threw off his garments heedlessly, extinguished the lamp, and crept into the ready hiding-place. (pt. II, ch. iv, 194–95)

The first paragraph emphasizes the hero's attempt to dissociate himself from his own shameful conduct. He regards it as "what had happened" rather than what he had caused to happen. He remembers it as "a mad dream"—something that surged up from his unconscious mind rather than from his conscious will. But although this waking "dream" strikes him as "mad"—contrary to his usual rationality—it also has a "ludicrous coherence." Though he wishes to brush aside his contemptible masquerade as merely laughable, it makes all too much sense. His alternate explanation, "somnambulism," resembles yet differs from dreams: a somnambulist walks within the real world but without any perception of it. Yet Peak has hardly functioned as an unknowing sleepwalker, for he has told self-serving lies and worn fake expressions. He attempts to explain his purposive behavior as the result of some "extraordinary influence," a mysterious force beyond his own control. In denying that "his conscious self had" performed any "part in" this disgraceful "comedy," Peak shifts his metaphors away from dreams to theatrical make-believe. "Taking count of the character he had played," he finds his role comic, yet he also insists that he acted it unawares. But this strange excuse raises an inevitable question: who, then, wrote the script?

The next paragraph gives a very odd answer. Peak himself wrote the script, but he did so long before he finally acted it out. During its enactment he forgot his own script yet also stuck faithfully to it. And when he first composed this farce, he did not think it comic, for it embodied his deepest frustrations. He saw his role then as despicable but not at all funny. He even toyed with the notion of assuming the role for life.

The concluding two paragraphs at last admit a connection between the man who wrote the script and the man who played it out. Here Peak judges himself in very harsh terms: "cowardly," "craven," mean, blustering, "weak," "idle." Yet the word "instinct" suggests a last feeble excuse: a powerful inborn impulse to cheat. Still, he need not have acted upon that impulse, so that he cannot, after all, escape the blame. In his final admission of disgrace, he derides even his own reflection in the mirror. He creeps to bed in order to hide his guilt in the dark oblivion of sleep—an ironic reminder of his first excuse that he had acted in a dream. In collapsing, however, into his psychic hiding place, the hero avoids the only course of honor still available to him: telling the Warricombes the truth. Here and throughout most of *Born in Exile*, Gissing achieves an intense yet subtle portrayal of corrosive bad conscience within a skeptical mind—a mind that doubts the validity of even its own shame. Although the book remains firmly grounded in external social details, it also probes the inward human reality of consciousness itself.

Chapter Five

Anatomies of Mismarriage

During the years in which Gissing's second marriage turned sour, he wrote three long novels that stressed the ills of wedlock: *The Odd Women* (1893), *In the Year of Jubilee* (1894), and *The Whirlpool* (1897). Although each contains much of Gissing's special brand of disillusioned realism, all share a weakness that he had avoided in *New Grub Street* and *Born in Exile*: a central male character inadequately judged by the story's narrator. In an 1897 essay on Gissing, H. G. Wells called these figures "exponent" characters because of their exclusion from narrative criticism.[1] Wells did not say, however, just what the "exponents" expound: in *The Odd Women* and *Jubilee*, an unobjectified grudge against women and marriage; in *The Whirlpool*, a disguised expression of this very same grudge, as the saintly hero endures his wife's egoistic vagaries until at last he regrets not having restricted her freedom like an old-fashioned husband.

The Odd Women

The revived feminist movement has renewed critical interest in *The Odd Women*.[2] And, in fact, the novel's most impressive sections deal compassionately with the single females or "odd women" relegated to a world of second-rate jobs. But scenes involving these "odd women" take up less than half the book. The larger portion emphasizes instead the male-female pairings of both courtship and marriage.

The first seven chapters and scattered later ones depict the sufferings of "the odd women" with both sympathy and authentic social detail. The six Madden sisters provide the central examples of unfortunate single females. Their father has given them genteel educations but dies without leaving them a large enough income to support genteel ways. Within ten years three have suffered early deaths, and three struggle on in ill-paid and degrading work: Virginia as a lady's companion, Alice as a governess, and Monica as a drapery saleswoman. Soon the two oldest sisters can find no jobs at all, and the youngest and most attractive, Monica, begins to lose her health from oppressively long working hours. Two possible means of relief present themselves to Monica: a feminist clerical school run by Rhoda Nunn and Mary Barfoot, or an aging but well-to-do suitor, Edmund Widdowson, whom Monica has met in a public park. With little enthusiasm Monica tries the school but soon leaves to marry Widdowson, whom she does not even like. In this opening third of *The Odd Women*, Gissing achieves an almost naturalistic realism unmatched in English fiction except perhaps by George Moore's *Esther Waters* (1894).

In chapter viii, however, the "exponent" male enters—Mary's cousin Everard Barfoot—and begins to damage the story's air of authenticity. The narrator and even the feminist characters express great admiration for this grumbler about the stupidities of women, this complacent pleasure seeker who has retired at twenty-nine to become a full-time world tourist. A romantic debate develops between Everard and Rhoda, an advocate of feminist celibacy; he proposes a "free union,"[3] but she demands a formal marriage. Gissing handles this conflict of the sexes like material for a light comic novel. Neither character really cares about the subject of their argument, yet each seeks the other's submission as a demonstration of love. Everard at last gives in, but then the courtship collapses when a tricky plot device causes the heroine to suspect him unjustly of having an affair with Monica. When this muddle finally ends, the lovers have exchanged debating positions. Everard now insists on a formal marriage and Rhoda on a "free union." As a result, she rejects him and he marries someone else. This symmetrical dance of courtship belongs to another world than the one in which the Madden sisters nearly starve to death.

Gissing depicts the Widdowson-Monica marriage far more skillfully than the Barfoot-Rhoda courtship mainly because of a willingness to judge Widdowson's faults: a chauvinistic belief in masculine wisdom as opposed to female childishness, a stupifying rigidity of habits, a frightened shrinking from all social intercourse, and a jealousy approaching paranoia. The ultimate marital breakup, however, comes about through a rather clumsy twist in the plot: two male candidates for adultery with Monica—Barfoot and a young man named Bevis—live in flats just below and above one another. Widdowson suspects the wrong man, Barfoot, and has a hired detective trail Monica, but, by knocking at the wrong door, she deliberately misleads him. The resulting tangle of misunderstandings and mistaken accusations belongs to a wholly different mode than do the earlier parts of *The Odd Women.* Even the conclusion of the Widdowson-Monica story seems discordant with the novel's feminist elements. Sexually disgraced without quite committing adultery, Monica dies in childbirth and thus conforms to the respectable Victorian narrative rule: erring women expire at the end.

Apart from Gissing's inappropriate plots about courtship and marriage, he undercuts even his moving portrayal of struggling workingwomen simply by introducing Barfoot as an "exponent" male who preaches a gospel of laziness and lives on interest and dividends. "Why," he asks, "is the man who toils more meritorious than he who enjoys?" (ch. viii, 82). Although Barfoot's retirement at only twenty-nine for a life of world travel expresses the author's own daydream (ch. viii, 77, 78, 82, 86), this fictional wish fulfillment clashes with the gospel of work as proclaimed by his liberated heroines, Miss Barfoot and Miss Nunn. They conduct a feminist vocational school to train women for jobs previously open only to men.[4] These feminists regard meaningful jobs as essentially character-building instead of the mere means of earning a living. "I am not chiefly anxious," Miss Barfoot tells her students, "that you should *earn money*, but that women in general shall become *rational and responsible human beings*" (ch. xiii, 135). She advocates, in fact, the work ethic of the high-Victorian era, proclaimed by such sages as John Ruskin and Thomas Carlyle. These arch-Victorians believed that work developed natural talent, released latent energy, encouraged systematic effort, combated narrow egocentricity, and taught self-discipline—the ability to defer pleasure for worthwhile future achievements. Amid the nineteenth century's declining faith in God, work could serve as a substitute religion, an ennobling earthly duty, and even a way of making sense out of an incomprehensible universe. In this religion, earning money and making goods took a secondary place to the work process itself, a strenuous process of soul saving.[5]

Gissing's feminist leaders accept the Victorian belief in work, with only one amendment. They insist that the sphere of jobs for mid-Victorian women—cook, cradle rocker, governess, hospital nurse—remained too narrow to permit full salvation (ch. iv, 37; ch. xiii, 136). But so-called unfeminine occupations will allow women to become "strong and self-reliant and nobly independent!" (ch. xiii, 136). Like the mid-Victorian preachers of the work ethic, Miss Barfoot rejects the old aristocratic notion that people with wealth should do nothing at all.[6] Although she has inherited "a modest fortune" (ch. vi, 54), she continues to toil for "the joy of advance," "the glory of conquering," the "winning" of "souls," the "propagation" of "a new religion," the "purifying" of "the earth" (ch. viii, 87). Yet when Everard Barfoot, the perpetual world traveler, enters with his Pater-like doctrine of "a ceaseless exercise of all one's faculties of pleasure," even Mary Barfoot, after some slight grumbling about "Satan and idle hands" (ch. viii, 82), confesses to Miss Nunn that "my cousin is a fine specimen of a man, after all, in body and mind" (ch. viii, 87). Miss Nunn agrees about the impressive "quality of his mind," and she finds "his talk . . . sympathetic" (ch. xiv, 148). Gissing fails to convince the reader that these hard-working feminists would empathize in the slightest with an egoistic male who lives only for sybaritic pleasures.

Young Barfoot worked only so long as he lacked the money for full-time tourism: for endless saunters through Japan, Egypt, Turkey, France, and Italy (ch. viii, 77, 78; ch. xviii, 190–91). Now, living in idleness, he still has an annual income of £450 (a comfortable one on a late-Victorian scale), yet he complains that this "pittance" leaves him "wretchedly poor" (ch. ix, 89; ch. xvii, 178). Not even the complication of a typical Gissing will—Everard's father left Miss Barfoot "much of" the legacy expected by the son (ch. viii, 84)—can make us believe that she would sympathize with his difficulty in supporting rich habits (ch. viii, 84–86). And his complacent satisfaction at his later inheritance from a conveniently dying brother—"Everard could now count upon an income of not much less than fifteen hundred a year" (ch. xviii, 188)—contrasts almost obscenely with the odd women's miseries. For example, the unemployed Alice and Virginia plan a desperation budget of "fourteen shillings and twopence a week." " 'Is such a life worthy of the name?' asked Virginia in tones of awe" (ch. ii, 14).

As a further incongruity, the book's other chief male character, Edmund Widdowson, also loathes and rejects the work ethic. Not only has he retired at forty-two on an annual income of some £600 (ch. v, 41–44), but he considered his former job "a hideous fate" (ch. v, 43). Yet he worked as a clerk, precisely the occupation for which Mary Barfoot trains emancipated women: "Because I myself have had an education in clerkship, and have most capacity for such employment, I look about for girls of like mind, and do my best to prepare them for work in offices" (ch. xiii, 135). As the present author has written elsewhere, "the contradiction seems extraordinary: clerkship, a living hell for men and a feminist salvation for women."[7]

Although Gissing respects the feminist gospel of work, he exempts his males from this mid-Victorian faith. As a result of his bitterness toward his second wife, he now believed that admirable men far outnumbered admirable women. By Barfoot's calculation, "a million or so" splendid males stand over against "perhaps a few" thousand splendid females (ch. x, 102). In other words, most women still require salvation by work, but Gissing's "very intelligent and highly educated" men can safely do nothing and do it very well (ch. x, 102). In *The Odd Women*, in short, Gissing's considerable sympathy with the feminist movement remains essentially ambivalent because of the opposing aims of his masculine egoism.

Long after one has forgotten the novel's "exponent" male, one remembers the moving struggles of its unattached women to retain a sense of worth. A single scene stands out with particular poignancy—that in which Virginia, the secret alcoholic, is first discovered drunk by her sisters:

> "O Virgie! What *does* it mean? How *could* you?"
>
> "Go to bed at once, Virginia," said Monica. "We're ashamed of you. Go back into my room Alice, and I'll get her to bed."
>
> Ultimately this was done. With no slight trouble, Monica persuaded her sister to undress, and got her into a recumbent position, Virginia all the time protesting that she had perfect command of her faculties, that she needed no help whatever, and was utterly at a loss to comprehend the insults directed against her.
>
> "Lie quiet and go to sleep," was Monica's last word, uttered contemptuously.
>
> She extinguished the lamp and returned to her own room, where Alice was still weeping. (ch. xxviii, 304)

Virginia's drunkenness represents a pitiful retreat from soul-saving labor—specifically from Miss Nunn's suggestion that Virginia open a school along with Alice (ch. iii, 24). For a temporary illusion of gin-soaked well-being, Virgie abandons the effort to achieve self-reliance and self-worth. In their different ways, each sister recognizes that alcoholism is a calamity for a self-respecting woman: Virginia's pathetic denial that she is hopelessly drunk, Monica's anger, and Alice's tears. One underlying element makes the scene extraordinarily touching: the humiliated Virginia, the angry Monica, and the tearful Alice all care deeply about one another and about each other's good opinion. Their mutual concern seems a universe away from Barfoot's self-centered "exercise of all" his "faculties of pleasure" (ch. viii, 82). These compassionate descriptions of "the odd women" largely justify Walter Allen's praise of the book: "one of the very few novels in English that can be compared with those of the French Naturalists."[8]

In the Year of Jubilee

Like *The Odd Women, In the Year of Jubilee* attempts to treat problems of courtship and marriage yet suffers from Gissing's distorting resentment toward his second wife. The double standard for judging men and women becomes particularly marked in the final volume, which he himself confessed to his friend Eduard Bertz "is not of a piece with what comes before."[9] But in volumes I and II, the vitality of Nancy Lord, the heroine, at least partly compensates for this weakness. And the many satiric portraits of nouveau-riche vulgarity provide still further compensation in a flawed but lively novel.

In this novel, which swarms with misogynous vignettes of vile and foolish women, Nancy offers a partial exception as a problematic heroine with much brash ignorance but also with potential wisdom. At the start, she encounters three possible suitors: a quoter of snippets from his daily newspaper, Samuel Barmby, Jr.; a shrewd but uncultivated advertising agent, Luckworth Crewe; and a haughty poor relation of a rich commercial family, Lionel Tarrant. She rejects Barmby, encourages Crewe, but flirts with Tarrant until he seduces her. Without her knowledge, however, the heroine's ailing father has decided to disinherit Nancy or her brother if they wed before their middle twenties. After Nancy secretly marries Tarrant, her father dies, and she learns of his will and its surprising prohibition.[10] When Tarrant himself loses an expected inheritance, the couple resolve to conceal their wedlock so that Nancy can preserve her immediate allowance and also her ultimate legacy. When the heroine learns that she has become pregnant, they decide upon a secret birth. Yet her husband feels such disgust at this new complication that he sails off without her to the Bahamas for a long-term business venture. Although the narrator comments about Tarrant's self-absorption, one detects

Gissing's not-so-sneaking sympathy with his hero's wish to flee from both marriage and fatherhood.

Nancy gives birth in seclusion. But her husband remains overseas and fails to reply to her message that he has become a father. When her friends and acquaintances learn of the heroine's concealed maternity, she accepts the shame of being thought an unwed mother in order to hide her marriage. Virtually abandoned by Tarrant, she develops remarkable strength of character.

When Tarrant at last returns, the novel changes abruptly into a male-chauvinist fantasy. This seems all the more surprising in view of the powerful Ibsen-like scene in which Nancy rebukes her contemptible husband: "I shall never forgive you for the way in which you have behaved to me. . . . I should never acknowledge you as my husband."[11] Yet once he apologizes, she not only forgives him but grovels before his supposed masculine supremacy. She agrees to his demand that they keep separate lodgings, and she accepts his occasional conjugal visits as a great husbandly favor. Although they forfeit Nancy's legacy, her brother conveniently dies and leaves her half his wealth. In the book's closing pages, Nancy bows to Tarrant's final decree that they never spoil their ideal marriage by actually living together. A revealing detail confirms one's impression that Gissing has indulged in a wish-fulfilling ending: Tarrant, like his creator, becomes a professional writer.

The subplots derive vitality from Gissing's marital resentment of women. Fanny French tortures the heroine's brother by foolish promiscuity. Mannish Beatrice French displays unpleasant brutality. And the screaming shrew Ada French Peachey torments her mild-mannered husband. One particular episode carries a bitter conviction unsurpassed in Gissing's domestic scenes: after having driven a petty-thieving housemaid into cutting her own throat, Mrs. Peachey insists on prosecuting the poor wretch and accuses innocent Mr. Peachey of an affair with her. When that good-natured husband flees his hateful marriage with his child in his arms, the contrast with wife-deserting Tarrant seems far more damaging to the hero than Gissing probably intended.

Throughout *In the Year of Jubilee*, Gissing's portrayal of contemporary society expresses a satiric repugnance more intense than anything in his earlier work. Like the book's essay-writing protagonist, Lionel Tarrant, Gissing seems to have turned to "the kind of composition which now came most easily to him,—a somewhat virulent sarcasm" (III, pt. V, ch. v, 85). In its strongest parts, *Jubilee* depicts the boorish offspring of parents who have themselves climbed from humble and uneducated families into middle-class comfort. The specific young vulgarians dissected here live in Camberwell—a south-London suburb quickly expanding with nouveaux-riches arrivals.[12] The novel focuses upon the means by which their children seek improvement in manners and taste. Because these human products of rapid social change do not know the middle-class rules for talking, thinking, dressing, home decorating, or even for amusing themselves, they take instruction from what we now call the "mass media." From advertisements these uncultured citizens learn the proper goods and services to buy: "theatres, journals, soaps, medicines, concerts, furniture, wines, prayer-meetings" (III, pt. V, ch. ii, 37). From the words of popular songs, Gissing's unsophisticates draw a sentimental vocabulary for love making (III, pt. VI, ch. i, 164). And, of course, they have also attended formal schools that have explicitly tried to refine their cultural rawness (I, pt. I, ch. ii, 14).[13]

The book's title comes from the 1887 celebration of Queen Victoria's fiftieth Jubilee—a celebration that dominates "Part the First: Miss Lord." The Jubilee itself appears in these pages as another mere mass entertainment, a royal offering to the tastes of the London mob. Yet Victoria's day of honor also becomes an advertising status symbol, as shrewd entrepreneurs propose or market "a Jubilee Perfume," "a Jubilee Drink," and "a Jubilee Fashion Club."[14] Gissing, however, does not view his consumers of mass culture with a cool sociological eye. His descriptions of them seethe with contempt. And he saves his strongest sarcasm for females (particularly for wives) rather than for males. Even the ambivalent feminism of *The Odd Women* gives way here to barely qualified misogyny.

Consider a passage from *Jubilee* that illustrates both its satiric strength and its distorting male bias. In this description from volume I, the narrator emphasizes Nancy's lack of cultural discrimination as she gazes at advertisements in an underground train:

> Sitting opposite to Samuel, she avoided his persistent glances by reading the rows of advertisements above his head. Somebody's "Blue;" somebody's "Soap;" somebody's "High-class Jams;" and behold, inserted between the Soap and the Jam—"God so loved the world, that He gave His only-begotten Son, that whoso believeth in Him should not perish, but have everlasting life." Nancy perused the passage without perception of incongruity, without emotion of any kind. Her religion had long since fallen to pieces, and universal defilement of Scriptural phrase by the associations of the market-place had in this respect blunted her sensibilities. (I, pt. I, ch. vii, 106–7)

Here the narrator, but not the heroine, ridicules the cultural jumble fostered by mass advertising—a jumble that equates profit-motivated slogans with appeals to the human spirit. "Somebody's" bluing, soap, or jam = God's Son. A message about a household product = the gospel of eternal life (John 3:16). The narrator criticizes Nancy for her bland acceptance of these absurd and debasing cultural equations. He explains her insensitivity not only by her loss of religious belief but also by her having become accustomed to advertising's constant juxtapositions of the banal and the sacred. Gissing's sharp satirical attack on this cultural leveling process places him in an important tradition stretching from Wordsworth and Carlyle to such twentieth-century critics of the mass media as Aldous Huxley, George Orwell, and innumerable other social and political commentators.

Within the context, however, of the novel's marital themes, this criticism of Nancy's taste appears skewed by masculine resentment. Throughout the book Gissing judges the cultural failings of his female characters far more harshly than those of his males. Advertising agent Crewe, although a promoter of vulgarity, nevertheless acts like a decent human being. The uncultivated commercial man Peachey, a junior partner in a dishonest firm, remains a kindly father. Even that pompous half-literate, Samuel Barmby,

Jr., shows a certain generosity toward the humilitated Nancy. And Nancy's foolish brother seems corrupted mainly by infatuation for the worthless Fanny French. Among the novel's men, only Tarrant displays an intrinsic and thoroughgoing selfishness, but Gissing excuses his "exponent" male primarily because he likes good literature (see, for example, I, pt. II, ch. v, 219). Yet the culturally naive heroine has far more human appeal than the aesthetically fastidious hero. Like the book's handling of marriage, the satire against mass culture suffers distortion from the novelist's own private marital resentments.

The Whirlpool

Lacking *The Odd Women*'s scenes of naturalistic compassion or *Jubilee*'s angry flashes of satire, *The Whirlpool* has less vitality than either of its predecessors, but it hangs together better as a whole. Although melodrama dominates this story of fashionable extramarital intrigues, it ranks as Gissing's most effective attempt at a sensational plot. Yet, because of one basic peculiarity, the overall effect differs from ordinary melodrama: Gissing's hero, Harvey Rolfe, stands curiously detached from the lurid events around him. Amid the thrills of ruined reputations and unnatural deaths, he remains a meditative stoic with impeccable good manners. Even when faced with his own wife's doom, this protagonist seems little more than a coolly uninvolved spectator.

In the novel's opening chapters, the crash of the Britannia Banking Company damages all the characters except prudent Harvey Rolfe, a bachelor who has declined to invest in it and who calmly observes the ruin of his unwise friends. Among them, the sportsman Hugh Carnaby and his elegant wife, Sibyl, go abroad to hide their straightened means. The Britannia heiress herself, beautiful Alma Frothingham, suffers not only from her father's loss of wealth, but also from his disgrace and his lurid suicide. She attempts to build a professional career out of limited talent as an amateur violinist, but Rolfe rescues her by proposing marriage, and they move to rural Wales.

For two whole years, Rolfe overlooks his wife's flighty inadequacies, but her sudden hysterical outbreak persuades him at last to humor her by returning to London's fashionable "whirlpool." Through her returned friend Sibyl, Alma now enters a scandalous demimonde, which Rolfe fastidiously ignores. He remains unaware of a growing sexual rivalry between his wife and Sibyl for the financial favors of Cyrus Redgrave, a libertine millionaire. Redgrave invests in a business bought by Sibyl's husband Carnaby, but the millionaire also supports Alma's self-indulgent whim of performing as a concert violinist. Rolfe feels increasing annoyance at Alma's neglect of their boy yet remains wholly uninvolved in her approaching catastrophe. Carnaby finds Alma and Redgrave together; mistakes her for Sibyl; and, in a jealous rage, unintentionally kills the philanderer. Innocent of actual adultery, Alma persuades poor Carnaby not to mention her presence as a witness. In spite of her shock, she gives an acceptable concert, which Rolfe does not even deign to attend. Carnaby receives a two-year prison sentence but expresses his gullible faith in his wife's sexual fidelity.

Meanwhile, Alma's behavior grows increasingly erratic, yet Rolfe holds apart from her troubles, philosophizes about marital unhappiness in general, and seeks comfort in loving his son. When Carnaby leaves prison and learns that Alma has gossiped about his wife's sexual guilt, he finally tells Sibyl about Alma's presence at Cyrus Redgrave's death. In revenge, Sibyl divulges the secret to Rolfe. Alma collapses in hysterics, but he treats her apparent infidelity with his usual detached kindness. Anguished that she cannot ever prove her innocence, she dies from a morphine overdose. Freed at last from marriage's distractions, Rolfe takes his boy to a small country town and a life of meditative calm.

In *The Whirlpool*'s fictional world, the decline of traditional values has corrupted both private and public life—both the realms of family and business. The Britannia Company's collapse in the book's opening chapters sounds the basic theme. Gissing's portrayal of a financial crash may owe something to the Overend and Gurney failure (1866), the City of Glasgow Bank debacle (1878), the House of Barings crisis (1890), and perhaps also Augustus Melmotte's fictional bankruptcy in Anthony Trollope's *The Way We Live Now* (1874–1875).[15] After the Britannia's collapse, both male protagonists take dangerous business risks on their own. Carnaby buys into a gold-mining process and also a bicycle factory.[16] Even prudent Rolfe invests his cash in a photographer's shop, though he knows nothing about the business and though his active partner, young Morphew, has behaved unreliably till now. For once, Gissing uses the essential ill fit between his characters and their occupations to make a valid social point. He depicts a post-1860s economic period epitomized by the rise of joint-stock companies with limited liability. In place of the old-fashioned patriarchal owner who knew his business thoroughly, control often passed to directors with wealth, high position, or perhaps personal influence but with little knowledge of the firm or its trade.[17] Within Gissing's novel, commerce has no socially redeeming value but remains merely a means of increasing income for citizens with money to invest. Both Carnaby and Rolfe would prefer to do nothing, yet eventually they attempt to guard their capital by watching over the businesses in which they have sunk cash. For these would-be men of leisure who have run short of funds, the work ethic has little relevance. Indeed, both the honest businessmen and the frauds who fill the novel (banking swindlers, gamblers, high-society blackmailers, and West End burglars) aim single-mindedly at maximizing profits rather than at building character through worthwhile labor. Significantly, however, behind Gissing's depiction of money-mad husbands, lies a not-so-hidden misogyny. All these men feel driven by the urgent need to support spendthrift wives with fashionable tastes.

Ironically, the book's working husbands struggle amid a world of business corruption in order to support wives who have themselves become equally corrupt. Misogyny expresses itself more subtly here than in *Jubilee*, for *The Whilrpool* deals with essentially polished women. Yet throughout the novel, the mid-Victorian dream of "Home, Sweet Home" as a peaceful family enclave, a refuge from cutthroat commerce, a domestic heaven with a lovely female angel, turns into a late-Victorian nightmare.[18] Nevertheless, Gissing's husbands doubt their right to criticize their wives. These males tend, in fact, to share their wives' assumption that the whole duty of woman consists in self-expression. Alma neglects her child, but Rolfe withholds criticism out of respect for her womanly freedom. Carnaby's icy wife remains childless and also despises her own mother, but this self-deprecating male considers himself unqualified to judge Sibyl's elegant manners and mores. Both Alma and Sibyl regard their homes as merely transient lodgings, and both deny their husbands the rural peace that they crave. Yet each man permits his wife to dictate the family's fundamental lifestyle. Shirking household duties, Alma attempts to build a professional career out of only minor musical talent, but Rolfe defends her freedom of choice. Sibyl seems exclusively concerned with her elegant social image as one of London's high-society beauties. Yet although Carnaby feels uncomfortable with her fashionable friends, he suppresses all his objections. Alma toys with adultery and Sibyl apparently commits it, and both consider it little more than a practical expedient—a means for gaining money and social favors. Yet each husband makes adultery all too easy by allowing his wife to sleep away from home whenever she wishes. In short, the novel depicts masculine surrender to female independence as calamitous for home and family.

In a brief but highly significant digression, Gissing underscores his antifeminist theme by praising the traditional virtues of one Mrs. Morton, a small-town wife and mother:

> ... In these little ones she saw the end and reason of her being. Into her pure and healthy mind had never entered a thought at conflict with motherhood. Her breasts were the fountain of life; her babies clung to them, and grew large of limb. From her they learnt ... the sweetness and sincerity wherewith such mothers, and such alone, can endow their offspring. ... She would have felt it an impossible thing to abandon her children to the care of servants; reluctantly she left them even for an hour or two when other claims which could not be neglected called her forth.[19]

Of all the women in the novel only Mrs. Morton receives unmixed praise. This "pure and healthy" mother stays at home, minds the babies, and remains a "fountain of life," "sweetness," and "sincerity." The contrast with the novel's hostile portrayal of emancipated wives seems even more striking when one recalls *The Odd Women*'s female reformers. In just four years, Gissing had moved from an ambivalent sympathy toward feminism to a surprisingly strong resentment against its basic assumptions.

Chapter Six

Four Short Novels

By the middle 1890s a changing literary market forced Gissing to turn to short one-volume novels. Until then he had worked within the three-volume form prevalent in England for over half a century. But just when he had achieved his masterpieces in this genre—*New Grub Street* and *Born in Exile*—the literary demand for three-decker novels began to melt away. Since 1842 the fiction market had depended upon a system of commercial lending libraries, dominated by Mudie's. These libraries rented out expensive new novels purchased from the publishers at very substantial discounts. The three-volume high price kept the public from buying directly but guaranteed the publishers a steady, dependable sale to the book-rental houses. By the late-Victorian period, however, free public lending libraries and cheap one-volume books threatened this whole cozy arrangement.[1] By 1891 firms like Gissing's new publishers, Lawrence and Bullen, sought one-volume novels for direct sale to the readers. Gissing obliged Lawrence and Bullen with *Denzil Quarrier* (1892) but then returned to the three-volume form in which he excelled. On 27 June 1894, however, the bottom dropped out of the three-decker market; Mudie's and its chief rival, W. H. Smith's, announced a policy of discouraging the no-longer-profitable three volumes in favor of shorter fiction.[2] Gissing duly noted this announcement in his *Diary* (3 July 1894, 341), and, in the following year, he published three one-volume novels in succession: *Eve's Ransom* (1895), *Sleeping Fires* (1895), and *The Paying Guest* (1895).

Unfortunately for Gissing's work, this change came about just when he had achieved his highest proficiency at the three-volume form. *New Grub Street* uses its three-decker expansiveness to multiply the problem of struggling writers into numerous parallel cases—Reardon, Milvain, Yule, Miss Yule, Biffen, Whelpdale—each of which sheds light on the others. And *Born in Exile* takes advantage of its three-volume space to unfold slowly and carefully the complex mental development of its protagonist, Godwin Peak, from schoolboy to middle-aged hypocrite. Now Gissing had to compress his expansive art into short single volumes.

Regrettably, he, like many other Victorians, considered the one-volume novel an inferior form, suitable for light comedy or sensational melodrama.[3] His attitude resembled that of his character Edwin Reardon in *New Grub Street*: "But this time he was resolute not to undertake three volumes. The advertisements informed him that numbers of authors were abandoning that procrustean system; hopeless as he was, he might as well try his chance with a book which could be written in a few weeks. And why not a glaringly artificial story with a sensational title?" (*New Grub Street*, ch. xii, 168). Indeed, Gissing tended to regard the short novel as essentially a stripped-down three-decker. In two of these mininovels—*Denzil Quarrier* and *Eve's Ransom*—he even retains inappropriate elements of a double plot, the favorite Victorian device for constructing three-volume narratives. As a result, Gissing's short novels seem significantly inferior to his other ventures into compressed fictional form—his numerous short stories. *Denzil Quarrier, Eve's Ransom, Sleeping Fires*, and *The Paying Guest* are somewhat too attenuated for full-scale novels and rather too dawdling for brisk short fiction.

Denzil Quarrier

Denzil Quarrier amounts to little more than a potboiler, although the materials might have made for a serious narrative. Gissing wrote this short book in only thirty-eight days during a time when he felt upset by the difficulty of finding a publisher for

Born in Exile.[4] In contrast to that novel's unrelenting honesty, *Denzil Quarrier* seems to palter with the issue of moral relativity. The book centers around the nemesis resulting from the hero's pretended marriage to a woman trapped in wedlock. Less than eight years after writing *Denzil Quarrier*, Gissing feigned a marriage to Mlle Fleury under rather similar circumstances but without either remorse or nemesis.[5]

As the narrative begins, the independently wealthy Denzil Quarrier and frail clinging Lilian enjoy domestic contentment in a secret love nest. But, as we later learn, the two cannot marry because of her unfortunate wedlock to a sleazy ex-convict. Unwisely, however, the hero introduces Lilian to his friend Eustace Glazzard, a dilettante artist with shady moral tendencies. Still more unwisely, Quarrier decides to run as a Parliamentary candidate in the provincial town of Polterham, but he attempts to avoid political scandal by introducing Lilian as his just-married bride. Nevertheless, he tells the entire secret to Glazzard, who himself wished to run for Parliament in Polterham and consequently now hates his supposed friend. As a further problem, the town's militant feminist, Mrs. Wade, feels disappointed at this "marriage" because she wanted Quarrier for herself. Out of villainous envy toward the hero, Glazzard tracks down Lilian's husband, Northway, and pays him to cause a scandal. Northway approaches Lilian with Mrs. Wade also present, and thus the feminist learns that Quarrier remains legally unmarried and, theoretically at least, available for herself. She pretends to help the heroine but, in fact, does everything possible to drive her out of her wits. On Mrs. Wade's advice, Quarrier bribes Northway to keep silent. But when the ex-convict attempts further blackmail, Mrs. Wade goads Lilian into drowning herself in a nearby pond.[6] Because the sexual scandal remains undisclosed, the hero wins the election. In a final vain effort to gain Quarrier's sexual gratitude, the feminist uncovers Glazzard's hidden treachery and reveals it to the horrified protagonist.

In contrast to the impressive sense of actual political processes achieved by Anthony Trollope's many fine Parliamentary novels, *Denzil Quarrier*'s political details seem essentially "faked," in E. M.

Forster's sense of the term—based upon fantasy rather than upon any knowledge or even intuition of how actual politics works.[7] Gissing presents his hero as a Radical-Liberal candidate for Parliament in 1880, the year in which Gladstone led the Liberals to victory against Disraeli's Conservatives by campaigning against an imperialism that had suffered a recent setback in Afghanistan.[8] Although Quarrier remains an aggressive imperialist at heart, he runs on the anti-imperialist side.[9] And although he has an aristocratic temperament, he passes himself off as a Radical or social reformer: "Of course I could speak just as strongly on the Conservative side with regard to many things" (ch. iii, 31–32). Yet Gissing makes little of these obvious contradictions. Instead, he treats them as the essential characteristics of a successful virile politician. The novel, in fact, portrays politics as little more than oratorical word spinning—the creation of rousing speeches out of random political stuff: "Certainly he had the gift of speech . . ." (ch. vii, 71); ". . . he could not speak otherwise than vigorously, and at times his words were eloquent" (ch. vii, 78); "it was true that he had discovered his vocation; he spoke like a man of long Parliamentary experience . . ." (ch. xv, 167). Indeed, Gissing's politician hero seems a hack writer in disguise who aims at the vote market rather than the literary one.[10]

In handling the ethics of the hero's pretended wedlock, the novel itself displays a similar opportunism, a calculated appeasement of the home-and-family reading market. The story's moral debates carry hardly more conviction than the protagonist's political speeches. At one point, Quarrier defends his sham marriage with an argument that Gissing quickly knocks down: "Social law is stupid and unjust, imposing its obligations without regard to person or circumstance. It presumes that no one can be *trusted.* I decline to be levelled with the unthinking multitude. You and I can be a law to ourselves" (ch. ix, 101). The "you" addressed in this "you and I"—the second-rate artist Glazzard—promptly betrays his friend's compromising secret. And soon after the hero's declaration of independence from the conventional masses, a wise philosophic character defends them: "Without tolerably honest fools, we should fare badly at the hands of those who have neither wit nor honesty. Let us encourage them, by all means. I see no dawn as yet of the millennium of brains." This philosopher calls "honest fools" "the pillars of society," echoing the title of Ibsen's play but not his indignant irony (ch. x, 114).[11] In the novel's final sentence, Quarrier concedes his earlier mistake in believing that "the millennium of brains" had arrived: "Now I understand the necessity for social law!" (ch. xxvii, 308). Yet the novel has raised the claim of moral privilege for genius in a way that never permits the reader to take the issue seriously. Because Gissing gives neither hero nor villain the slightest gleam of brilliance, the superman argument seems wholly out of place. Even as a mere thirty-eight-day production, this trifling book appears unworthy of Godwin Peak's creator.

Eve's Ransom

Although Gissing wrote *Eve's Ransom* almost as rapidly as *Denzil Quarrier*, he, in fact, based his second one-volume novel upon a much longer work called "The Iron Gods," a three-decker of his tossed aside a year before with all but twenty pages written. "I am using as much as possible of my old Birmingham story," he declared in his *Diary* (19 April 1894, 335).[12] Indeed, the original title appears in *Eve's Ransom* as a phrase spoken by the hero: "I am no longer slaving under the iron gods. I like my work, and it promises to reward me."[13] In discussing his plan for the three-volume novel, Gissing had once explained that "The Iron Gods" (or a variant title, "The Gods of Iron") referred to the way that industrial machinery turned workers themselves into mere "machines."[14] In *Eve's Ransom* Hilliard regards himself as a "living machine" condemned, as a draftsman, to sketch "damned" machinery (ch. vi, 94; ch. iii, 34). The bookkeeper heroine, a frustrated tabulator of other persons' money, first worked for a Dudley ironmonger (ch. iv, 52–53). And the eloquent descriptions of Birmingham and Dudley as places very like Hell draw upon Gissing's trip of 1892 to investigate those industrial towns.[15] As a further connection with his "Iron Gods" manuscript, Gissing's narrative describes the protagonists' escape from their bondage to mechanized commerce. His adaptation of materials from the longer, discarded work may have helped him achieve a certain polish in this quickly written novelette.

Eve's Ransom has a simpler plot than any previous novel of Gissing's. Perhaps for this reason, he utilizes the Jamesian device of presenting everything from the hero's point of view—a method that delays our full comprehension of the not-very-complex events until the hero himself comprehends them. In the first two chapters, Hilliard receives £436 from a debt owed to his late father. Hilliard immediately quits his Dudley job and resolves to live for pleasure as long as the money lasts. He flees the Black Country, vacations in Paris, but then returns to England to look up Eve Madeley, a pretty woman whose picture he had seen back in Dudley. He finds her in London, apparently at leisure yet showing signs of overwork. He also gradually discovers that she has entangled herself with a married man. The hero whisks Eve away to Paris, chaperoned by her common but good-natured friend, Patty Ringrose. When Hilliard and the heroine return to the Birmingham-Dudley region, she grudgingly agrees to marry him but only when he can earn enough money to provide her with middle-class comforts. Meanwhile he has obtained an apprenticeship as an architect, through the influence of his best friend, Narramore, a bedstead manufacturer. But Hilliard does not know that Eve has met Narramore and has drawn a marriage proposal from him too. Though she lacks the courage to break with her old suitor, she all but accepts his secret rival, who remains ignorant of the hero's prior claim. When Hilliard finds out what she has done, he explodes in righteous anger, but, at last, with surprising generosity, he smooths her way to marry the richer man. By the novel's end, the hero has succeeded as an architect, and the heroine has gained material contentment as a well-off suburban wife.

Eve's Ransom deals rather honestly with an obsession that had distorted much of Gissing's earlier fiction—premature retirement from work for a life of travel and leisure. The ironic story of Hilliard's seven-month escape from "the iron gods" seems far more grounded in social reality than do similar escapes in, say, *The Odd Women.* The English sociologist T. H. Marshall has noted how the old land-owning ideal of aristocratic leisure based on unearned income evolved into the professional one of dignified work based on freedom of choice—work that "did not dull the brain, like manual labour, nor corrupt the soul, like commerce." Marshall has also pointed out that eventually even the nonprofessional businessman could "pay apparent homage to the older ideas by purchasing complete idleness for his wife. . . ."[16] Because of sharply limited funds, Hilliard (and, through him, Eve) can enjoy merely a few leisured weeks in Paris. In the end, though, the hero ascends from the routine work of a simple mechanical draftsman to an architect's professional freedom: "And Maurice Hilliard, a free man in his own conceit, sang to himself a song of the joy of life" (ch. xxvii, 379). Through marriage with her well-to-do businessman, Eve herself achieves a modest suburban counterpart of the aristocratic ideal, or, as Hilliard puts it, she becomes "comfortably settled for life" (ch. xxvi, 370). In contrast to Gissing's earlier fantasies about globe-trotting young retired males, *Eve's Ransom* describes a lower-middle-class world where leisure can be achieved only by hard work or by a cynical marriage for cash.

The temporary leisure that Hilliard provides for Eve raises the book's central question: what, if anything, does she owe him for this gift? Before she met the hero, she had herself received a £20 reward for returning a lost cash box. She used the money to treat herself to more than a month of theatergoing idleness (ch. xvi, 228–32). But the £20 ran out before she could recover her good health, and she had to find work again. At this point, Hilliard enters with his £436. He insists upon using his money to take her to Paris and also to pay for a chaperone. He ransoms Eve from her depressing new job, although hardly with a queen's ransom, for he can afford only a moderate middle-class one. He acts partly from generosity, partly from loneliness (he has earlier felt unhappy during six solitary weeks in Paris—ch. v, 61, 63), and partly from a wish to get something in return. Hilliard refrains from demanding immediate sexual payment because he hopes that Eve's gratitude will eventually persuade her to accept him as a husband. From his point of view, he has sacrificed much for her: he has run through money that he had hoped would last for two full years of leisure and must return to work after only seven months (ch. iii, 39). But from Eve's point of view, Hilliard expects lifelong devotion in return for a summer vacation. Narramore, by contrast, has the instant means to provide her with a perpetual vacation in suburbia. Not surprisingly, she takes the better offer. Gissing emphasizes the conflict between Hilliard's wounded feelings and his cost-accounting admission that he has asked too much for the services that he has rendered.

In a passage apparently derived from "The Iron Gods" manuscript, the narrator's description of Eve's old Dudley neighborhood helps to explain her drive to achieve material comforts:

> Indescribable the confusion of this toilers' settlement—houses and workshops tumbled together as if by chance, the ways climbing and winding into all manner of pitch-dark recesses, where cats prowled stealthily. In one spot silence and not a hint of life; in another, children noisily at play amid piles of old metal or miscellaneous rubbish. From the labyrinth which was so familiar to her, Eve issued of a sudden on to a sort of terrace, where the air blew shrewdly; beneath lay cottage roofs, and in front a limitless gloom. . . . (ch. xviii, 259–60)

In this depressing community where Eve grew up, dwelling places and work places exist side by side in the same urban squalor. The absence of street lighting epitomizes the general lack of middle-class amenities. In this town of industrial metallurgy, the very children play amid heaped-up "old metal"—a sign of pervasive manufacturing blight. And the "limitless gloom" suggests a depression of the spirit as well as simple physical darkness. Toward the story's close, Narramore promises the heroine one chief marital perquisite: a house in the country with "a tree or two about" (ch. xx, 279–80; ch. xxiii, 329), a middle-class Eden for an Eve who has known only urban sordidness. Yet even with this excuse for her, Gissing's depiction of his mercenary female makes for a cold little novel. He employs an abstraction known as *economic man* but transforms it into *economic woman.*

Sleeping Fires

Gissing wrote *Sleeping Fires* in only forty-six days, and he himself considered it a "paltry little book."[17] The entire story builds to the ultimate admission by the aristocratic heroine that she should not have rejected the hero for having fathered an illegitimate child. Yet the debate between his enlightenment and her benighted prudery seems far too one-sided for effective narrative tension.

At the opening, the "English gentleman" Edmund Langley encounters young Louis Reed at Athens in the company of the boy's paid traveling companion.[18] Langley learns, to his surprise, that Louis's legal guardian is the fashionable widow, Lady Revill, who had years before rejected the hero's marriage proposal because he confessed to having an illegitimate son. Louis complains of estrangement from Lady Revill caused by her new suitor, Lord Henry Strands: this imperious aristocrat has forbidden correspondence between Louis and a middle-aged and married philanthropist, Mrs. Tresilian, whom the boy much admires. Langley returns to England to plead Louis's case with Lady Revill. In reply, she startles the hero by identifying her ward as his own illegitimate child, a discovery that she had up till now concealed. But before the paternally moved Langley can return to Greece and reveal himself to his son, news comes that Louis has suddenly died. Bitterly, the hero rebukes Lady Reville for having needlessly kept his child from him out of mere prudish disapproval. Yet Langley soon begins a second courtship of Lady Revill and at last persuades her to marry him more than twenty years after first having rejected him. Gissing, however, avoids playing out the scene of the heroine's climactic surrender. She accepts the hero in a letter, whose words Gissing does not even report. Indeed, the novelist hurries through this conventional happy ending as though he felt embarrassed by it.

In spite of its attacks on sexual prudery, *Sleeping Fires* also aims at snob appeal by exploiting the conventions of the high-society or the "silver-fork" school of fiction. During the writing of this silver-fork romance, the novelist recalled a reader's complaint about the depressing poverty of the typical Gissing character: " 'Oh,' said someone to Bullen [Gissing's publisher], 'do ask Mr. Gissing to make his people a little better off!' "[19] In *Sleeping Fires* he made them much "better off." The wealthy hero has graduated from Cambridge, served as a Peer's private secretary, and received a large "legacy of which he stood in no need..." (ch. iii, 27–29). The heroine represents "the very best type of aristocratic woman," with vast sums of cash that have mellowed for generations in the family's safes and vaults (ch. i, 9; ch. iii, 31). When she breaks with the hero over his confession of having fathered a bastard son, she marries a local baronet and Member of Parliament (ch. iii, 33, 40). Upon becoming widowed in early middle age, she considers an all-but-"royal" marriage to Lord Henry Strands, whose noble title far outshines the mere commoner's rank of baronet (ch. iv, 53–55; ch. xii, 176, 181). By finally agreeing to marry the untitled Langley, Lady Revill, in fact, displays true noblesse oblige.

In contrast to the opening chapters' vivid Athenian background drawn from Gissing's diary account of his 1889 trip (chs. i, ii, iv, v, vi),[20] the subsequent background of English high society seems unconvincingly vague. In Athens, for example, a small circumstantial detail particularizes the dusty scene, as a hotel waiter brushes Louis "from head to heel—a necessary service performed for all who entered" (ch. ii, 17).[21] But in England Langley enters Lady Revill's Kensington home amid a haze of indefinite wealth and imprecise magnificence:

> The door opened, and solemnly, behind a solemn footman, he ascended the stairs, vaguely percipient of the marks of wealth and taste about him, breathing a fragrance which increased the trouble of his blood....
>
> A murmur of the footman's voice; a vision of tempered sunlight on many rich and beautiful things; a graceful figure rising before him. (ch. vii, 92–93)

The only concrete nouns are "door," "footman," and "stairs." The rest remains generalized. Not even "the trouble of" Langley's "blood" can reconcile this hazy evocation of fashionable splendor with the vividness of scenes in Athens. In this hastily written fashionable novel, the author's silver seems merely silver plated.

The Paying Guest

Although *The Paying Guest* must rank as basically minor Gissing, it comes off as light entertainment. Gissing wrote the actual story in only two weeks, after two months of abortive beginnings.[22] But he may have drawn upon his discarded pages, for the book seems too polished for a mere fortnight's work. Indeed, *The Paying Guest* succeeds quite well in its mildly comic vein, though Gissing achieved more impressive comedy within the short story—a form that he used more frequently than the short novel.

The novel centers around the comic conflict between the Mumfords' fearful gentility and Louise Derrick's spirited vulgarity. Out of a need for money, Mr. and Mrs. Mumford rent a room to Louise in their red-brick suburban cottage with the grandiose name of "Runnymede," but they insist upon calling her a "paying guest" instead of a mere cash customer. Although they feel contaminated by a visit from Louise's *h*-dropping mother, they decide that they can bear the daughter because she, at least, "sounds her *h*'s."[23] Louise has a working-class suitor named Cobb yet hopes, through the Mumfords, to meet men of somewhat higher status. In actuality, however, the Mumfords' tiny social circle includes only people exactly like themselves—tense upholders of money-pinched refinement. A crisis arises when Louise's stepfather withholds her rent money to punish her for flirting with his own daughter's suitor. In response to Mrs. Mumford's practical suggestion that Louise should now go home, the young woman stalks angrily from the house. Later, however, she persuades Mr. Mumford to intervene for her with his wife. As a result, "the paying guest" stays on temporarily, but Mrs. Mumford now begins to seethe with jealousy. Only when Louise's artisan lover promises her a house just like

"Runnymede," does she finally agree to marry him. Yet before she can leave her lodgings, she and Cobb quarrel about her past behavior. As the two lovers scuffle, they accidentally knock over a paraffin lamp and set the house on fire. Before Cobb can put out this drawing-room fire, it burns and chars the Mumfords' silly knickknacks—their emblems of domestic propriety. But Louise marries her workingman, and he pays for the paltry damages, and they even send a wedding card to the still-shaken Mumfords.

This little book stands as Gissing's only novel that successfully makes light comedy out of English class distinctions. The amused tone contrasts with his usual bitterness about petty-bourgeois and proletarian vulgarity, as, for example, in a letter written only a few months before *The Paying Guest.* "My books," he told Morley Roberts, "deal with people of many social strata. There are the vile working class, the aspiring and capable working class, the vile lower-middle, the aspiring and capable lower-middle, and a few representatives of the upper-middle class."[24] *The Paying Guest* avoids this invidious classification of various "social strata" into two opposing receptacles labeled vile and capable. Significantly, however, the heroine belongs to the same suburban nouveaux riches whom Gissing had bitterly satirized in *Jubilee*: "Louise Derrick represented a certain stage of civilization, a degree of conscious striving for better things . . ." (ch. i. 20). But unlike his earlier study of how such women torment thin-skinned males, *The Paying Guest* keeps its vulgar heroine in almost complete isolation from cultured middle-class suitors. Because she remains segregated from men like Gissing himself, he can smile at her frustrated efforts to marry above her station. Although Louise hints broadly at her wish to meet genteel male friends of the Mumfords, they feel "uneasy as to the impression this guest would make upon their friends" (ch. ii, 37–38). Mr. and Mrs. Mumford make only one nervous and halfhearted attempt to introduce Louise to a marriageable young man—a stockbroker's clerk named Bilton—but he snubs her with contempt (ch. iii, 57–60). Later, his barely suppressed sniggers help convince the Mumfords that they have demeaned themselves by admitting Louise into their respectable circle. Finally, their "paying guest" relieves their mortification by marrying within her own social station.

In a key passage, the narrator explains why Louise Derrick can live happily ever after only by marrying an artisan with a grease-stained hat: "In talking with Cobb, Louise seemed to drop a degree or so in social status; her language was much less careful than when she conversed with the Mumfords, and even her voice struck a note of less refinement. Decidedly she was more herself—if that could be said of one who very rarely made conscious disguise of her characteristics" (ch. vi, 124–25). In other words, with her own social equal, Louise does not have to suppress her own authentic voice.

This observation reminds one of Dr. Henry Hick's opinion that working-class Edith, Mrs. Gissing number two, "would doubtless have made a good wife to a man in her own station."[25] One wonders whether Hick derived this opinion from Gissing himself, for, indeed, the doctor and the novelist renewed their schoolboy friendship just before Gissing wrote *The Paying Guest*.[26] The novel may owe its essentially genial humor to Gissing's fantasy wish that his second wife had, in fact, married someone—anyone—other than himself.

Chapter Seven

An Erratic Diversity

Gissing's last five novels seem anticlimactic epilogues to his distinguished achievements in long fiction. Perhaps because of his declining health after 1896,[1] Gissing did his best work in short stories, criticism, vivid descriptions of travel, and meditative essays—genres that allow for shorter creative bursts than is possible in long fictional narratives. And his worsening illness may have sapped the energy that he needed to meet changing novelistic fashions.[2] In any case, the novels that close his career appear remarkably diverse—a heterogeneous batch of full-length odds and ends. They include a Cockney farce, an idealized love story, a satirical comedy, a romance of grocery life, and a historical melodrama about declining Rome. Much of this miscellaneous fiction lacks the true Gissing flavor, the shabby-genteel realism that marks his finest books.

The Town Traveller

The Town Traveller (1898) aims at broad Cockney farce. It may owe something to Dickens, whom Gissing was reading at the time, and still more to H. G. Wells, a new personal acquaintance, whose *The Wheels of Chance* (1896) Gissing had recently read.[3] He noted in his *Diary* one specific passage where Wells contrasts the comic contentment of his own Cockney hero with Gissing's typical characters: "... His real life was absolutely uninteresting, and if he had faced it as realistically as such people do in Mr.

Gissing's novels, he would probably have come by way of drink to suicide in the course of a year. But that was just what he had the natural wisdom not to do."[4] Wells's comment could serve as a gloss for Gissing's shift from the suicidal gloom of *The Whirlpool* (1897) to an attempt at perpetual hilarity. And his justification for *The Town Traveller*'s farce to his ex-publisher Bullen provides still a further gloss: ". . . I *must* make money. . . ."[5]

The Town Traveller has an absurdly intricate plot—one that seems less comic than confusing. The Cockney salesman or "traveller," Gammon, becomes amorously involved with two related women: Mrs. Clover and her niece Polly Sparkes. Many years previously Mrs. Clover's eccentric husband abandoned both her and her daughter, but he keeps sending them money from an unknown London address. Niece Polly, a playhouse usher, has seen the missing husband come to her theater with two unknown women. Gammon tracks down Clover with the help of a clue from the amateur genealogist Greenacre: Francis Quodling, a London businessman strongly resembling Clover, is the bastard child of one Lord Polperro. At Quoding's office, the hero glimpses the long-vanished husband (not to be confused with his businessman look-alike) and finds that he has become the present Lord Polperro.

Gammon tells his discovery to Polly and urges her to trail one of the women who first appeared with Polperro at the theater and has since returned alone. Polly has her other suitor, Christopher Parish, track the woman to a West End mansion. But when Gammon and Polly summon Lord Polperro to a showdown, Greenacre comes instead as the lord's representative. Desperately ill, Polperro finally visits the abandoned Mrs. Clover, but he hints to Gammon at the distressing possibility of another low-born wife. The lord burns his will in order to replace formal bequests to Mrs. Clover and her kin by secret deeds of gift, but he dies before drawing them up—yet another example of Gissing's obsession with the old-fashioned plot device of tangled inheritances. Meanwhile, Gammon tells Mrs. Clover that she married a man who later became a lord, but Greenacre now reveals that the marriage was bigamous, though Polperro's legal wife has long since died. As consolation prizes for lost bequests and titles, Polly marries Christopher Parish, her persistent suitor, and Gammon marries Mrs. Clover. Throughout all these plot gyrations, the jolly Mr. Gammon sniggers, chuckles, cackles, laughs, and roars with highly exaggerated delight.[6]

Although *The Town Traveller* attempts broad farce, the narrator undercuts it by frequent disgusted grumblings about his Cockneys' liking for dirt and vulgarity. The book's opening pages set the dyspeptic tone with a long description of bad "lodging-house smells," including "the ever-rising vapours from a sluttish kitchen."[7] And the narrator later notes Polly's habitual pleasure at this same kitchen's "dirt and disorder" (ch. vii, 64). He emphasizes the unpleasant "dust and sweat" of a south London thoroughfare but adds that Polly finds it "cheery and inviting" (ch. i, 6). Similarly, Gammon loves dirty eating-houses with badly cooked food: "Sweet to him were the rancid odours; delightfully familiar the dirty knives, the twisted forks, the battered teaspoons; not unwelcome the day's newspaper splashed with brown stains of coffee and spots of grease" (ch. v, 42). The commentary also notes a wine shop's raucousness and its "stifling" air but insists that "no such" objections could occur to Gammon or his friends (ch. viii, 75–76). In short, the book tends to split into two distinct realms of perception: the jolly viewpoint of insensitive Cockneys and the disgust of the all-smelling narrator. At one point, he actually compares Gammon's self-contentment to that of a happy horse or dog (ch. xii, 116). And the narrator also contemptuously describes "the muddled obscurity of Polly's consciousness" (ch. vi, 56).

The reason for this hyperfastidious commentary seems obvious enough. Unlike Louise Derrick in *The Paying Guest*, Gammon and Polly feel complete satisfaction with their habitual working-class ways. Unlike Louise, they do not yearn for middle-class improvement. As a result, although Gissing aimed at Cockney humor, he could barely conceal his distaste for his material. *The Town Traveller*, he grumbled to Gabrielle Fleury, "is a vulgar book and therefore has sold better than any of my others."[8]

The Crown of Life

The Crown of Life (1899) represents a surprising return to the immature "idealism" that Gissing had renounced many years before. His regression undoubtedly sprang from his recent meeting with Gabrielle Fleury, whose clear superiority to his now-estranged wife renewed old erotic fantasies. Just four days after he first met Gabrielle, he was "thinking" of "The Crown of Life," and five days later he had written a tentative beginning.[9] Both in his love letters to her and in the novel itself, "ideal" keeps reappearing as a magical verbal sign to induce the desired emotions. Consider, first, a sentimental passage to Gabrielle and then, just below it, a similar passage from the novel:

> After all, ought one not to be thankful for the soul of an idealist? Now that you love me, I can feel glad of these qualities in myself, and I feel able to speak of them quite simply, without arrogance.[10]

> He looked forth upon the world, its activities, its glories, and behold, there was for him but one prize worth winning, the love of the ideal woman.[11]

These passages typify the frequent invocations to the sentimental muse in both the letters and the novel. In Gissing's first rush of love letters to Mlle Fleury, he called her my "ideal of womanhood," "the ideal of a passionate heart," an "ideal," and "my own ideal of personal beauty."[12] In the novel itself, the word *ideal* and its variants appear even more frequently—at least twenty-one separate times—in praise of the noble-hearted heroine and hero and of spiritualized love in general.

Gissing's story splits humanity into two opposing camps: a vast unfeeling mass incapable of amorous spirituality and a small elite with the "genius of love" (ch. xx, 185). The illegitimately born young man, Piers Otway, has soulful erotic faith, unlike the worldly characters around him, including his two half brothers, the selfish Daniel and Alex. When the hero encounters beautiful Irene Derwent, he falls so deeply in love with this "ideal woman" that he can no longer prepare for his impending Civil Service examination. Meanwhile, Daniel and Alex take turns at bilking the hero of his rather small savings. And Alex disgraces Piers with Irene Derwent by getting him drunk in public. The crushed young man flees to a business career in Russia but continues to worship Irene from afar. He seeks to gain wealth enough to win her respect. His beloved father, however, dies, so that the bastard hero loses his anticipated inheritance, and the legimate heirs fail to repay their old debts to Piers.

The hard-working hero finally resolves to propose to Irene. But before he can speak, she becomes engaged to one Arnold Jacks, an imperialist politician. Meanwhile, Irene's aunt faces a blackmail threat from Piers's vicious half brother Daniel. Although the aunt dies of brain fever, Piers nobly saves her honor by paying the cynical Daniel to return her amorous and compromising letters. Amid various peripheral plot complications, Irene breaks off her engagement to Jacks because she does not love him. After eight years of distant worship, the hero at last proposes marriage to his "ideal woman," and she gratefully accepts him.

The historical subtheme of *The Crown of Life*—pacifism versus imperialism—is weakened by the sentimental framework. In the period covered by the book, 1886–1894, the British Empire expanded throughout Africa, and imperial rivalries between European powers intensified their warlike nationalism. With the off-stage character Trafford Romaine, Gissing provides a fictional counterpart of Cecil Rhodes (1853–1902), the controversial leader of British colonial Africa.[13] And in this time of war scares between the major powers, Gissing makes his hero ardently pro-Russian. On page after page, he and the other admirable characters preach world brotherhood, and the detestable ones advocate military aggression. One may admire the novel's politics yet dislike its stilted debates. In fact, Gissing's depiction of Piers's enlightened views has an embarrassingly sentimental function: to demonstrate the hero's nobility in international politics as well as in domestic eroticism.

The novel's portrayal of romantic love seems less an "ideal" than a sexual daydream. On page one the hero indulges in a voyeuristic fantasy, as he gazes at shop-window pictures of beautiful women: ". . . His eye . . . was drawn irresistibly to the faces and forms of beautiful women set forth with varied allurement. Some great lady of the passing time lounged in exquisite array, amid luxurious furniture lightly suggested; the faint smile of her flattered loveliness hovered about the gazer; the subtle perfume of her presence touched his nerves; the greys of her complexion transmuted themselves through the current of his blood into life's carnation; whilst he dreamed upon her lips, his breath was caught, as though of a sudden she had smiled for him, and for him alone" (ch. i, 1). In describing the shop-window prints, Gissing emphasizes the unmistakable signs of high female status: "great lady," "exquisite array," "luxurious furniture." Like many actual Victorian males including Gissing himself, Piers cannot separate sexual attractiveness from distinctions of social class. Thus, even in mere pictures, only truly fashionable women can appeal to his erotic tastes. Undoubtedly, the scene reveals far more about the subsequent love story than Gissing consciously intended. The same daydream sexuality continues throughout Piers's self-absorbed and distant worship of the supposedly flesh-and-blood heroine. After the indulgent sentimentality of this book, Gissing virtually abandoned a lyrical eroticism for which he had little talent.

Our Friend the Charlatan

Jacob Korg has called *Our Friend the Charlatan* (1901) "a reworking of the problem of *Born in Exile* on a far lower level," and his remark has much validity.[14] Both novels deal with a dishonest hero, yet *Born in Exile* does so with a subtlety that contrasts with *Charlatan*'s rather broad farce, at times too reminiscent of Meredith's *The Egoist* (1879). From another viewpoint, however, *Charlatan* provides a satirical reworking of *The Crown of Life*'s sentimental daydreams. Specifically, *Charlatan* satirizes Gissing's "exponent" males, whose gentlemanly manners, superior minds, and brilliant eloquence win them ideal women, ideal wealth, and sometimes even ideal seats in Parliament.

Like *The Crown of Life*'s hero, *Charlatan*'s Dyce Lashmar considers himself a natural gentleman, a connoisseur of women, a spirit destined for achievement. But Gissing exposes the Oxford-trained Dyce as a lazy dilettante. In place of work or strain, he prefers donations from women. He lives, at first, on an ill-earned tutor's salary from one Iris Woolstan, a fluttery, aging, and adoring widow. When this sinecure ends, he finds another way of avoiding honest labor. He meets Constance Bride, an unglamorous former sweetheart who works for a philanthropic dowager in a small rural town. With Miss Bride's approval, Dyce appears there as a candidate for the town's Parliamentary seat. He bases his campaign on a political theory plagiarized from a Frenchman's sociological treatise.[15]

The withered old philanthropist, Lady Ogram, admires the hero's stolen ideas and offers to back him, although meanwhile he borrows cash from affectionate Iris Woolstan. He wonders which female to choose for his permanent source of money: plain Constance Bride, who will manage the Ogram philanthropies, or pretty May Tomalin, Lady Ogram's new-found grandniece and heiress apparent. The hero's furtive courtship of receptive May thwarts Lady Ogram's plan of marrying the grandniece to a poor but honorable lord and Dyce to Constance Bride. The furious dowager banishes her grandniece and demands the immediate marriage of Dyce and Miss Bride, but Lady Ogram dies before anyone can obey. Dyce resolves to marry whoever gets the wealth, yet, when May receives nothing and the hero proposes to the new philanthropic manager, Miss Bride scornfully rejects him. He also loses the election. Panic-stricken now, he marries the aging widow, only to learn on his honeymoon that her financial adviser has stolen much of her modest capital. In the splendid closing scene, the benevolently drunk husband forgives his adoring wife for running short of funds to support him in utter laziness.

Much of *Charlatan*'s satire revolves around a special historic circumstance of English political life: until 1911 members of Parliament received no pay. As a result, that body remained basically a rich man's club that excluded those who had to earn a living.[16] The hero's impoverished country-parson father complains to Dyce that "... you talk as if politics were a profession one could live by."[17] The Parliamentary campaign involves the moneyless hero in frantic maneuvers to find a female rich enough to support him. Although Dyce assumes that Lady Ogram will pay for his entire Parliamentary career, she believes him independently wealthy and offers to cover merely his campaign expenses—an arrangement that would leave him free to starve once he had won the election. In defiance of Lady Ogram's expressed wish, he shrinks from marrying plain Constance Bride "*without* a substantial fortune—that were disaster indeed!" (ch. xii, 153). He inclines toward May because she combines good looks with prospects of sufficient money to gild him into a fashionable M.P. In the final collapse of Dyce's Parliamentary plans, the election defeat itself seems a minor inconvenience after losing both potential heiresses. To move from the ridiculous to the Parliamentary sublime, one might contrast Dyce's ludicrous search for a wealthy political patroness with Benjamin Disraeli's financially convenient marriage to Mrs. Wyndham Lewis.[18] Significantly, Disraeli had a basic liking for women, but Dyce secretly despises them. Indeed, *Our Friend the Charlatan* provides a bitter indictment of male-chauvinist egoism—a relief from Gissing's sentimentalization of *The Crown of Life*'s hero.

Will Warburton

Like Harold Biffen's "Mr. Bailey, Grocer" in the pages of *New Grub Street*, *Will Warburton* (written from 10 July 1902 to 14 March 1903; pub. posthumously 1905) deals with a grocer's life and times.[19] This minor little novel achieves a certain charm, particulary when describing the hero's humble grocery store. Yet the book has only a surface resemblance to Biffen's attempt at "absolute realism in the sphere of the ignobly decent" (*New Grub Street*, ch. x, 150). Both Will Warburton's gentlemanly pregrocer background and the accompanying conventional love story fall into the realm of romance, as Gissing himself indicates by his subtitle—*A Romance of Real Life.*

He could hardly have called the book "Mr. Warburton, Grocer," for the hero has no grocerdom in his middle-class soul. He begins as a sugar-refining merchant, with wealth and position. He descends to humble shopkeeping only when his partner squanders all their capital, including money that Will has invested in the company for his mother and sister. The now-bankrupt hero becomes a grocer in order to continue the interest that his family expects and needs. But to save them from worry, he conceals his business troubles. When his secret finally emerges, he has won both honor and solvency through his lowly grocery store.

Will Warburton also contains a cheerful little love story—a much too cheerful one for "ignobly decent" realism. Unlike Biffen's Mr. Bailey, who marries a "big, coarse, squinting" woman for her cat's–meat–business money (*New Grub Street*, ch. xvi, 223), Will aims at true love. First, he becomes infatuated with the elegant Rosamund Elvan, the former fiancée of his friend Norbert Franks. But after she initially encourages the hero, she discovers his secret identity of grocer and flees in snobbish horror. Although he tries to pursue her, she hastily marries Franks in order to avoid the threat of grocerdom. Will quickly regains his senses and proposes instead to the admirable Bertha Cross, whom he has liked all along. This unpretentious heroine gladly accepts the grocer's offered love. She calls him "a very honest man—the most honest man I ever knew," and they live happily ever after.[20]

The book's most impressive parts deal with the mundane problems of Will's commercial life. Except for *New Grub Street* and its account of professional authorship, *Warburton* stands alone among Gissing's novels in emphasizing the process of earning a daily living. Though Gissing always stresses money's importance, his characters usually gain it by inheritance rather than work. This novel, however, centers around the minutiae of a businessman's profit and loss. The opening financial speculations of Will's sugar-merchant partner occur against a background drawn from late-

Victorian commerce: falling agricultural prices and persistent British refusal to enact a protective tariff (ch. iii, 19–22).[21] The whole novel hinges upon the resulting loss of the Warburtons' life savings—£4,000 belonging to Will's mother and sister, as well as slightly more than £4,000 of his own (ch. xiv, 85–88, 91–92). As grocer, Will aims at an annual profit of at least £120—the minimum needed to pay his mother's and sister's dividend (ch. xviii, 121). The chief narrative interest lies, not in the love story, but rather in the hero's efforts to squeeze the necessary earnings from a fairly humble business. Suspense arises out of simple accounting details. The grocery store's rent, equipment, stock, and also good will cost the hero £460, with still more cash needed to buy fresh food (ch. xviii, 120). To complete the transaction, he raises £660 from a still-intact bank account and from token repayments by his former partner (ch. xv, 101; ch. xvii, lll; ch. xviii, 117). Although the first-year profits end up too low, Will gains an additional £120 when Norbert Franks at last repays an old debt. As a result, the hero can provide his mother and sister with virtually the same interest that they would have gotten from his old respectable firm (ch. xxii, 144–45).

If the narrative at times suggests Will's discomfort at harsh retail competition, Gissing stresses his hero's ultimate commercial satisfactions. The book gets its flavor from small details of shop: "the grocery odours, . . . the weighing, parcel making, string cutting" (ch. xxiv, 162). One memorable passage describes Will's pleasure in handling the coins that he has earned in a day: "A gratifying aspect of the life was that, day by day, he handled his returns in solid cash. Jollyman's gave no credit; all goods had to be paid for on purchase or delivery: and to turn out the till when the shop had closed—to make piles of silver and mountains of copper, with a few pieces of gold beside them—put a cheering end to the day's labour" (ch. xxii, 144). The description of Will's delight in caressing his coins—an action usually typical of misers—remains, in fact, wholly sympathetic. Unlike the leisured males in many of Gissing's books, this hero has worked hard to earn his cash. In a humble way, this grocer protagonist embodies much of Gissing's own real courage in having supported himself and others for many years by steady, dogged writing.

Veranilda

In spite of Gissing's long fascination with sixth-century Rome, his classical romance about it seems an utter disappointment.[22] Yet one feels compunction in examining *Veranilda* (begun 1900–1901; resumed in 1903; pub. 1904) with too cold an eye. Both as he began it and as he tried to complete it, Gissing fell gravely ill. His death in December 1903 left the manuscript unfinished, with five concluding chapters missing.[23] This novel written in illness is filled with illness: the dying Maximus, the hero's uncle; the plague-agonized Petronilla, the hero's aunt; and the fever-ravaged hero himself.[24] The narrative, in short, smells of the sickroom.

Veranilda unfolds spasmodically, probably because Gissing's own increasing illness often interrupted this death-haunted work. The book centers around the devotion of the rich Roman Basil for the royal Gothic maiden Veranilda, yet their love affair begins offstage before the book has even started. Later this courtship develops against the historical backdrop described by Gibbon in *The Decline and Fall of the Roman Empire*, chapter 43: warfare (circa A.D. 546) between Justinian, the Byzantine Emperor, and Totila, the Gothic claimant to the Italian throne. Like Gibbon, the novelist considers the Goths far closer than their decadent rivals to the old Roman spirit.[25] In the midst of all this history, however, the narrative begins with a typical Gissing legacy. Although the dying Roman Senator, Maximus, grants his daughter, Aurelia, her full inheritance upon her renouncing the Arian church and returning to Roman Catholicism, his fanatically Catholic sister, Petronilla, conspires with the powerful Deacon Leander in order to deprive Aurelia of her wealth.

Meanwhile, the hero, Basil, journeys with Aurelia to his adored Veranilda, Aurelia's legal ward. Mysterious strangers, however, kidnap both women. Oddly enough, Aurelia drops from the story for good, without any further explanation. Basil suspects Petronilla of having abducted his love. He seeks help from his best friend Marcian, an influential Roman who serves as a double agent for both Totila and Justinian. But unknown to the hero, both leaders have asked Marcian to find Veranilda for their respective courts. At last, the secret agent discovers her in Deacon Leander's custody and impulsively resolves to have her for himself. Marcian falsely convinces the unsuspecting heroine that Basil has discarded her for another woman.

The now-ill hero learns of Marcian's treachery, tracks him down, and kills him in front of the terrified maiden. Unjustly, Basil accuses her of having become the villain's paramour. Fever-stricken, the hero recovers at Saint Benedict's own monastery, gains absolution for the killing, and repents of ever having doubted the innocent heroine—now, herself, under Totila's protection. Basil finally meets Totila, does brave deeds for him, and is promised Veranilda by the king. The book breaks off before the imminent happy ending, as the Gothic king blockades helpless Rome.

In spite of *Veranilda*'s historical trappings—its sixth-century tunics and cries of "by Bacchus"—the book regresses, in fact, to Gissing's abandoned idealism. *Veranilda* has a distinct social resemblance to his fashionable modern novels, such as *A Life's Morning* and *The Crown of Life.* The aristocratic Basil lives in gentlemanly leisure in his "great house" at Rome and his villa at Arpinum and concentrates on doing nothing (ch. vii, 74, 76). He knows all the eminent Romans but also becomes friendly with the august Gothic king. Furthermore, the other noble characters immediately recognize Basil's true nobility. And his love, Veranilda, has such angelic beauty that both king and emperor covet her. Yet, instead, this pure-hearted maiden chooses the "exponent" male: "As the sound trembled into silence, his lips touched hers. In the golden shadow of her hair, the lily face flushed warm; yet she did not veil her eyes, vouchers of a life's loyalty" (ch. vi, 64). In Gissing's own words from 1888, such idealizing passages are basically "poor stuff," whether in ancient Rome or nineteenth-century England.[26]

Chapter Eight
Short Stories

George Gissing's still-underrated short stories deserve to rank among the best of the late-Victorian era. He wrote some 110 in all, many very fine. Once he had mastered the art of brief narrative, it allowed him to break away from the wills, rival lovers, and theatrical climaxes that often clutter his novels. His finest short stories end, not with a melodramatic bang, but an ironic whimper. Yet even Gissing's admirers tend to ignore his impressive short fiction, perhaps because it has become rather inaccessible.[1]

Gissing's work in the short-story form falls into three distinct periods. First came the 1877 journeyman pieces written in America and the few additional ones from 1878 to 1882 that he wrote back in England but could not sell. Because they follow such mid-Victorian fashions as Poe-like horror and Dickensian moral sentiment, these pieces have little resemblance to Gissing's mature work. Yet these amateurish tales have autobiographical interest. Their fictional themes of guilt seem closely related to Gissing's own crime and punishment in Manchester.

After these early pieces, Gissing produced only three more short stories in the 1880s: "Phoebe" (written 1883; pub. 1884; rpt. *SS*, 15–44), "Letty Coe" (written 1884; pub. 1891; rpt. *SS*, 47–68), "Mutimer's Choice" (written 1884; pub. 1970 in *EF*, 242–53). All three deal with a lower-class milieu like that of the early novels. In "Phoebe" an artificial-flower girl finds a much-needed sum of money only to have it stolen by another proletarian woman whom the good-natured heroine has befriended.

In "Letty Coe" an accidental fire suffocates a costermonger's daughter, along with the donkey that he needs to earn his living. In "Mutimer's Choice" an injured workingman refuses to have his legs amputated, because he wishes to die and free his wife to marry the man whom she loves. Although these pieces display more skill than Gissing's earlier short fiction, they crowd too many calamities into too small a space for convincing emotional impact.

His most impressive proletarian short story came long after this period. "Lou and Liz" (1893; rpt. *VC*, 219–36) depicts the friendship of two working-girl roommates deserted by their men. Lou helps support both Liz and Liz's bastard child but considers herself superior until she learns that her own missing "husband" had committed bigamy with her. The subtle final scene of "Lou and Liz" shows how easily the resilient heroine gets over her chagrin at discovering herself unmarried. The whole piece reads like a correction of *Thyrza*'s idealizing softness.

By 1891 Gissing had perfected the art of short fiction. From then until his death, he wrote seventy-eight short stories, many of them remarkably fine. Their emphasis falls upon the lower middle class. A census of the fictional population of these mature pieces would include struggling writers and artists, traveling salesmen, shopkeepers, clerks, domestic servants, governesses, barmaids, and landlords. These pieces avoid the fault of the "exponent" male—that fantasy gentleman of leisure who inhabits Gissing's lesser novels. Above all, these stories emphasize an inextricable connection between social status and character.

Gissing's short fiction tends to center around one quintessential theme: the constrictive force of social class and narrow financial means upon aspiring men and women. Usually, the protagonists have shabby-genteel backgrounds and eke out livings in dreary or precarious work. The characters frequently clutch at an unwise marriage to escape from social frustration but find still more frustration as a husband or a wife than in unmarried loneliness. The plots hinge upon the characters' reactions to their straightened circumstances: trivial vexations, petty but stinging failures, ironically minor successes, and obscure struggles for a little self-esteem.

In these impressive yet understated pieces, Gissing shuns melodramatic twists. Instead his plot reversals remain fundamentally slight and subtle. An elderly governess saves just enough to buy a pathetically small retirement annuity ("An Old Maid's Triumph"—pub. 1895; rpt. *HOE*, 197–202). An overbearingly fastidious lodger marries his superneat landlady and finds that she nags him incessantly ("The Prize Lodger"—written 1895; pub. 1896, rpt. *HOE*, 133–54). An impoverished book collector destroys his wife's health by cramming dusty books into their tiny living quarters, and only her near death persuades him to renounce his beloved scruffy collection ("Christopherson"—pub. 1902; rpt. *HC*, 47–67). An up-till-now sheltered middle-class woman takes work as a mere housemaid, proudly masters her lowly duties, but finds herself trapped in them for life ("The Foolish Virgin"—written 1895; pub. 1896; rpt. *VC*, 187–216). A rebellious young daughter of a gardener and a housemaid defies their aristocratic employers but later must beg humiliating forgiveness to save her parents' jobs ("A Daughter of the Lodge"—written 1900; pub. 1901; rpt. *HC*, 175–91). Taken as a whole, Gissing's mature short fiction portrays the ironic comedy of shabby-genteel frustrations. A detailed look at a few of his very finest pieces may help to suggest his achievement in this genre.

"A Victim of Circumstances"

Gissing's first truly excellent short story, "A Victim of Circumstances" (written 1891; pub. 1893; rpt. *VC*, 3–36), resembles Henry James's tales of artists and writers[2]. Within Gissing's other works, *New Grub Street*'s many vignettes of shabby-genteel authors provide the closest parallels to this splendid short piece. "A Victim of Circumstances" deals with a straightened artistic couple, Horace and Hilda Castledine. The talentless husband thinks himself a Victorian Michelangelo, yet the truly gifted wife regards her own work as scarcely worthwhile. When a famous landscape painter happens to visit the Castledines' house, he shows contempt for Horace's vast amateurish canvas but admires Hilda's watercolor landscapes. The mortified husband pretends that he himself painted his wife's pictures. Meanwhile, in order to support the family, she has sold a few to a local art collector but concealed that she has painted them. When she learns of her husband's lie, she allows him to take the credit for her art rather than expose him to public humiliation. She resolves to sign all her future landscapes as H. Castledine, so that Horace can continue to say that he has done them. Eventually she perceives her husband's lack of talent, as well as her own undeniable gift. Yet when he gives up painting for full-time teaching, she abandons her own landscapes in order not to shame him by her steady artistic achievement. After her ultimate death, Horace continues to boast of "his" early watercolors. He laments having lost his talent but insists that he would have painted many great pictures except for the burden of two children and a wife.

Within the story as a whole, the ironic contrast between Horace's grandiose daubings and Hilda's modest watercolors rests upon actual deveolpments in nineteenth-century art. He attempts a form of academic history painting popular in the early Victorian period but already old-fashioned by 1869—the time of the story's beginning (*VC,* 6). He labors, specifically, at a huge canvas called *The Landing of Joseph of Arimathaea in Britain.* He claims that the finished picture will rival Michelangelo, Raphael, and Leonardo da Vinci (*VC,* 5–6, 9–11, 21–22).[3] She, on the other hand, works at unpretentious landscapes. Modestly, she considers herself a mere amateur, although the visiting painter suspects that, with a few years' practice, her watercolors might someday approach those of David Cox (1783–1859) and Copley Fielding (1787–1855), fine English artists if not Michelangelos (VC, 11–13, 18).[4] If her husband has studied anatomy (*VC*, 8–9), Victorian prudishness has blocked an artist such as Hilda from working with the nude, so that her choice of genres has remained somewhat limited.[5] But, ironically, Hilda's landscapes have far greater relevance than her husband's garish work to late-Victorian trends in painting. Ultimately, though, she must renounce all creativity in order to protect his unjustified self-esteem.

Significantly, however, this wifely renunciation does not bring Hilda old-fashioned marital bliss but, rather, smoldering frustration, which she hides from her egocentric husband: "No one divined what lay beneath her tender smile, with its touch of sadness—least of all Horace himself. No one knew of the long sleepless nights when she wept silently over a glorious hope that had come only to vanish. She had her moments of rebellion, but subdued herself. . . . An artist no longer, however her artistic soul might revolt, the duties of wife and mother must suffice for all her energies, and supply all her happiness" (*VC*, 31–32). The passage hints that a wife's creative ambitions have as much legitimacy as those of her mate. Even the consoling hope that Hilda may derive compensatory "happiness" as a dutiful "wife and mother" melts away in the sardonic epilogue. Her renunciation, we learn, has failed to preserve the family's well-being: her boy dies prematurely, her girl marries unhappily, and her husband debases himself by concealing Hilda's sacrifice even sixteen years after her death (*VC*, 36). His self-pitying bleat—"You can't imagine how completely an artist is at the mercy of circumstances" (*VC*, 34)—applies, ironically, not to himself, but to the remarkable woman whose talents he and society had thwarted by the doctrine of masculine supremacy.

"Comrades in Arms"

The delightfully wry "Comrades in Arms" (written 1893; pub. 1894; rpt. *HOE*, 1–19) stands as Gissing's most sympathetic portrayal of a so-called unfeminine woman, although it also has some connection with "The Poet's Portmanteau" (written 1893, pub. 1895; rpt. *HOE*, 74–91) as an attack on feminine stereotypes. At Wilfrid Langley's usual lunchtime restaurant, this under-thirty novelist encounters Bertha Childerstone, his "comrade in arms"—an over-thirty newspaperwoman who has just reviewed his latest book very favorably. The unmaidenlike Miss Childerstone boasts of having earned enough from her scribbling to equip a younger sister with a trousseau and dowry and send her off to marry a "soft-hearted" man in Natal (*HOE*, 3–4). But Langley perceives that Miss Childerstone has made herself ill through her selfless journalistic drudgery. He hurries her home in a cab and writes her next article for her. He provides a doctor and nurse and also a generous loan. As Miss Childerstone slowly recovers, he suddenly perceives her subtle attractiveness. But when he kisses this self-sufficient woman and then proposes marriage, she simply calls him "goosey" (*HOE*, 14). She promptly goes away without telling him where and refuses to see him again until they have "both recovered" (*HOE*, 17). As a sly suggestion that he also take a trip to cool down his sudden passion, she sends him "a large and handsome travelling-bag" (*HOE*, 18). He does travel abroad for a month, and then he and Miss Childerstone resume their old relationship as mere literary "comrades in arms."

The story emphasizes the spirited independence of its late-Victorian liberated heroine. Miss Childerstone takes pride not only in her professional career, but also in her role of substitute father for her conventional younger sister—specifically labeled "an old-fashioned girl, . . . an ideal housewife and mother" (*HOE*, 5). The emancipated woman journalist has resolved the basic tensions that Simone de Beauvoir found some fifty years later in twentieth-century career women. Unlike de Beauvoir's "independent" women, who accept the double burden of professional work and the feminine duty of maintaining a "scrupulously neat" home,[6] Miss Childerstone thrives in an untidy apartment strewn with books and newspapers. She herself connects her resistance to marriage with an unwillingness to dust and straighten like the usual domesticated female: ". . . I don't want to marry," she declares. "Look at this room, dirty and disorderly. This is all the home I care for" (*HOE*, 16, and see also 7 and 10). Unlike de Beauvoir's anxious professional women, Gissing's cheerful heroine feels no obligation to "do her own cooking" but goes to eat alone "at a restaurant as a man would in her place."[7] The story hinges, in fact, upon Miss Childerstone's unescorted encounter with the protagonist in a London restaurant. And unlike de Beauvoir's half-liberated women, Gissing's heroine feels no temptation to act girlishly and thus lure men by denying her superior "brain."[8] Indeed, Miss Childerstone teases and contradicts Langley with good-humored self-confidence. "Comrades in Arms" subverts the common belief that men must feel sexual repugnance for a genuinely masterful woman.

In an amusing passage toward the story's close, assembled party guests make fun of the absent heroine without knowing that the hero has become entranced with her:

> "Gone as war correspondent, I shouldn't wonder," said a young man; and the laughter of the company appreciated his joke.
>
> "Oh, she really is too mannish," remarked a young matron. "I suppose you study her as a curiosity, Mr. Langley?"
>
> "We're great chums," Wilfrid answered with a laugh. (*HOE*, 18)

The young man's ridicule of Miss Childerstone as probable war correspondent hints that she strikes him as an androgynous freak, a he-man in petticoats. And the young matron assumes that Langley can have only scientific interest in the apparently sexless heroine. But the hero's laughing description of himself and Miss Childerstone as merely "great chums" conceals the ironic truth: far from repelling him by so-called masculinity, she has had to fend him off, gently but firmly, to keep her contented independence.

"The Schoolmaster's Vision"

With its subtly ironic criticism of late-Victorian prudery, "The Schoolmaster's Vision" (written 1895; pub. 1896; rpt. *VC*, 127–44) achieves greater objectivity than another notable Gissing piece about sexual frustration—"A Lodger in Maze Pond" (written 1893; pub. 1895; rpt. *HC*, 241–64). As a preparation for his "vision," the headmaster of a second-rate school for boys, forty-year-old Mr. Donne, feels sexually aroused by Mrs. Argent, the young widowed mother of his pupil Willie Argent.[9] Fifteen years previously, Donne had settled for this mediocre job in order to marry his fiancée and provide for her. But she soon revealed herself as a mindless homemaker—the boring embodiment of high-Victorian propriety. At occasional guilty moments, he had daydreamed of supplementing his wife with a mistress, although Gissing avoids approval of Donne's adulterous thoughts by killing off Mrs. Donne long before the narrative starts. Previous to meeting Mrs. Argent, Donne thinks her selfish and neglectful because she has failed to visit her son. But when she finally does pay a visit, she whizzes in on a bicycle and captivates Donne by her emancipated manner, her spectacular good looks, and her daringly short skirts.[10] He conceals his lust, however, because of pedantic reserve but also because this wealthy young woman far outranks him socially. And before she rushes off on her bicycle, he has to confess that he does not even know how to ride one. The frustrated hero flees his campus and fails to return for the night. Instead, he takes a room at a small country inn and, alone in bed, experiences wildly erotic dreams.

Within his dream world, Donne miraculously rides a bicycle but cannot keep up with the cycling Mrs. Argent, who laughs at him scornfully. Then he sees her son weeping by the roadside, and, like the boy, the man begins to weep. Finally, his dream shifts to school, where Donne delivers a cynical harangue to a graduating student: beware of sexually dull and mindless wives. Upon awakening, the headmaster returns to his school and finds Mrs. Argent's son in actual tears. The boy has learned that his mother will remarry but will leave him in the care of an uncle. Donne comforts the boy with a falsely hearty speech about the character-building value of suffering. As the story ends, the hero seems as pompously donnish as ever.

Gissing makes his protagonist a schoolmaster because of the tendency of such academic authorities to indoctrinate the young in the sexual proprieties. Walter E. Houghton has noted how the most influential of all Victorian headmasters, Thomas Arnold of Rugby, felt obsessed by a need to eradicate schoolboy "sexual evil":

"dirty jokes, masturbation, . . . sodomy."[11] Unlike Rugby's Doctor of Divinity, Donne is "not in orders," but "he could on occasion discourse with the true clerical impressiveness," and Mrs. Argent, in fact, mistakenly called him "Dr." (*VC*, 131, 132). If his long "magisterial gown" symbolizes propriety (*VC*, 127), Mrs. Argent's short bicycle skirt represents sexual freedom. As she speeds unchaperoned along the public road, her cycling suggests the sexual act itself—an act from which Donne stands excluded. And her hedonistic refusal to play the role of mother contrasts specifically with Mr. Donne's belief that duties to "wife and family" have crushed his free spirit (*VC*, 140). Within his extended nightmare, the bicycle represents not merely sexual love, but a sexual love without entangling domesticity—an unrestrained eroticism that the hero cannot achieve even in mere dreams. Mrs. Argent complains of his unsuccessful efforts to keep up with her cycling: "Oh, can't you do better than *that*? You really must be quick; I can't wait for you" (*VC*, 138–39).

Written five years before Sigmund Freud's *The Interpretation of Dreams* (1900), Gissing's fictional dream stands somewhere between Freud and mid-Victorian medicine. Instead of revealing suppressed unconscious thoughts, Mr. Donne's libidinous "vision" builds to a large extent upon his conscious waking fantasies. His acute shame while dreaming reminds one of the moralistic psychology of Dr. William Acton (1813–1875), a mid-Victorian specialist in sexual disorders: "The *character* is the same sleeping or waking. . . . If a man has allowed his thoughts during the day to rest upon libidinous subjects, he finds his mind at night full of lascivious dreams. . . ."[12] In Gissing's story, Donne experiences a wildly erotic dream because he has loosened his censorship of his waking sexual fantasies. Consequently, he feels shame merely at having allowed the dream to happen. By the story's end, however, he recovers his control and delivers a hypocritical lecture on the virtues of sexual repression. In essence, Gissing accepted the mid-Victorian belief that the waking release of sexual longing led directly to libidinous dreams. But in contrast to upholders of repression, Gissing approved of sexual release both in life and dreams.

"The House of Cobwebs"

"The House of Cobwebs" (1900; rpt. *HC*, 1–27) offers a genial correction of the Bohemian-artist myth—the moneyless genius who defies social conventions and expands his creative gifts with sex, alcohol, drugs, and defiant nonconformity. This short story reminds one of *New Grub Street*'s many fine vignettes of unglamorous literary struggles. The story's young hero, the aspiring writer Goldthorpe, decides to take inexpensive rooms until he can finish his first novel. On a stroll through a south-London suburb, he notices three apparently abandoned old houses but discovers their proprietor in the back playing "Home, Sweet Home" on a concertina. This man, a retired drugstore clerk named Spicer, reveals that he owns the houses only under a short-term lease, and he also confesses that he himself lives in one of the dilapidated rooms. Honored at his encounter with an actual living author, Spicer offers the hero another of the broken-down rooms at a merely nominal rent. Goldthorpe moves in among cobwebs and smashed window panes and becomes Spicer's friend. The good-natured proprietor spends his time in the unweeded garden, cultivating scraggly flowers, assorted vegetables, and especially Jerusalem artichokes. Goldthorpe's book progresses while the summer remains mild, yet by sweltering August he falls ill in his unsanitary home. He finishes the book anyway, but a publisher rejects it. Discouraged, moneyless, and now quite sick, he creeps away to recuperate with his mother in Derbyshire. By winter another publisher at last accepts the novel, and Goldthorpe returns to London to tell his ex-landlord. In the meantime, however, Spicer has narrowly escaped death from a falling chimney stack in his crumbling "house of cobwebs." Although no longer able to live there, he feels comforted that the hero wrote his successful book "under my roof, my own roof, sir!" (*HC*, 27).

This account of a writer's triumph over poverty contrasts strikingly with a famous glamorization of late-Victorian Bohemianism, George Moore's *Confessions of a Young Man* (1886). Gissing himself considered Moore's *Confessions* "interesting but disgusting."[13] The wealthy Moore describes his exotic adventures as a painter-writer in Paris and London, in Montmartre and Curzon Street, amid fellow geniuses and delightful women. He boasts of his amorality, of his joyous acquaintance with demimonde rogues. Gissing's writer, however, stoically survives in a pathetic suburban hovel. He lacks artistic friends or female seductresses, and he behaves with a dull but scrupulous decency. In contrast to a well-born writer like Moore, who could leave Bohemia whenever he chose, Gissing's hero struggles against an encompassing beggary.

Although Goldthorpe, like most Bohemians, suffers from poverty, he makes no attempt to disguise it as a glorious way of life. When Moore describes his Bohemian apartment, he emphasizes expensively unconventional emblems: a terra-cotta faun, Turkish couches, a Buddhist altar, statues of Shelley and Apollo, incense burners and candles.[14] Gissing instead stresses his impoverished hero's commitment to simple household pleasures: possessing his own humble bed and table, cooking and sharing meals with his landlord, strolling through the run-down neighborhood, and smoking inexpensive tobacco out in the unkempt garden (*HC*, 13–14). If Bohemians tend to scorn middle-class life, Goldthorpe clings to it stubbornly. The song that first draws his attention to his shabby future lodgings—"Home, Sweet Home"—idealizes the virtues of nineteenth-century domesticity. One familiar line from the song sums up the story's central irony: "Be it ever so humble, there's no place like home." Amid cobwebs, smashed windows, collapsing chimney stacks, and a literally poisonous atmosphere, this typical Gissing writer touchingly adheres to respectable middle-class proprieties.

The four short stories analyzed above can help to convey the high achievement of Gissing's extensive work in this genre. If his novels range from the excellent *New Grub Street* and *Born in*

Exile to potboilers like *The Town Traveller* and *Sleeping Fires*, Gissing's mature short stories have an impressive consistency. His own characteristic version of the short narrative form suited his fundamental attitudes. Its inconclusive brevity seems particularly appropriate to his vision of human beings as fallible little creatures entangled in their petty social webs.

Chapter Nine

A Man of Letters

In his final years, Gissing shifted much of his creative effort away from pure novels to various other forms: literary criticism, a travel memoir, and a meditative journal assigned to an imaginary character. One cannot appreciate the writer's full achievement without reading these rich and mature late works. In 1941 Edmund Wilson called Gissing's critical writings on Dickens "the best things on" this novelist "in English." Shortly after Gissing's death, Edward Garnett praised *By the Ionian Sea* as Gissing's "most perfect artistic achievement." And in 1953 Cyril Connolly hailed *The Private Papers of Henry Ryecroft* as a "marvelous book."[1]

Dickens Criticism

Charles Dickens: A Critical Study (written 1897; pub 1898) received immediate acclaim. As a result, Methuen asked Gissing to supply the prefaces for a never-finished collected Dickens edition. Although Gissing actually wrote eleven, only six appeared in his lifetime, and the manuscripts of two unpublished prefaces have since disappeared. The posthumous *Critical Studies of the Works of Charles Dickens* (written 1898–1901; pub. 1924) brought together nine of Gissing's prefaces on Dickens along with another short piece on him.[2]

Gissing's essentially sociological criticism tends toward the panoramic: he examines social patterns that cut across individual works. Consequently, the thematically organized *Charles Dickens:*

A Critical Study ("His Times," "Women and Children," "The Radical," etc.) fits the critic's method better than prefaces can, dealing as they do with individual books. Yet the collected prefaces do contain valuable details that supplement the more tightly woven *Study*. In "*Sketches by Boz*," for example, Gissing singles out one striking simile to illustrate the lower-middle-class roots of Dickens's imagination. "Of a pleasure steamboat in a high wind it is said that 'every timber began to creak, as if the boat were an over-laden clothes-basket.' Who but Dickens would ever have hit upon a fancy so homely?"[3] And, one might also ask, what late-Victorian critic except Gissing would have noted the sociological basis of Dickens's figures of speech?

René Wellek's three broad categories for the sociological approach—"the sociology of the writer, the social content of the works themselves, and the influence of literature on society"—apply particularly well to Gissing's Dickens criticism.[4] Utilizing all three categories, Gissing explores the complex relationships between literature and society. He begins *Charles Dickens* by showing how the novelist's attitudes relate to his lower-middle-class background in the early nineteenth century—an era when the English bourgeoisie gained social and political power. Yet Gissing also notes anomalies in Dickens's social outlook: although Dickens identified strongly with the vitality of a rising capitalist class, he never forgave his bankrupt family for making him work at the age of ten to twelve in a lowly blacking factory. As a result, he developed strong sympathies for the socially oppressed, particularly for mistreated children. But he also strove to offset his early humiliations by becoming a wealthy gentleman.

In his sociological approach, Gissing displays considerable tact and balance. He confesses, for example, that Dickens's social background cannot itself account for the novelist's verbal genius, his gift for mimicry, his eye for rich details, and, above all, his exuberant humor. "Where else since Shakespeare," the critic asks, "shall we find such force in the humorous presentment of gross humanity?"[5] Gissing acknowledges a further complication in attempting to isolate social influence upon Dickens's fiction: literary and theatrical models that also helped shape the novelist's imagination. For example, the critic describes how Dickens's love of eighteenth-century fiction gave direction to his basic comic sense. Gissing, on the other hand, deplores Dickens's affection for popular Victorian drama, as encouraging stagy plots and exaggerated histrionics. Yet, at any rate, Gissing insists that literary and also theatrical influences must exert their effect within a social world. Thus, he connects the novelist's enduring kinship with Fielding, Smollett, Goldsmith, and Sterne to Dickens's limited education: he read them young and, as a grown man, failed to keep up with European fiction. And the critic suggests that Dickens's fondness for naive melodrama sprang from his unsophisticated petty-bourgeois background, his essentially common tastes.

In analyzing social patterns within the works themselves, Gissing denies the frequently made charge that Dickens draws mere eccentric caricatures. The critic offers a census of Dickens's fictional characters and finds that most reflect actual English types, largely from the lower middle class: bankrupts, law clerks, respectable hypocrites, ignorant housewives. Gissing, however, adds the important reservation that "Dickens never succeeded in depicting an ordinary well-bred and charming girl . . ." (*CS*, "*Nicholas Nickleby*," 67). At one point, though, in discussing Dickens's shrews, the unhappily married Gissing loses objectivity: he praises the paralyzing "blow on the back of" Mrs. Joe Gargery's head in *Great Expectations* as "a sharp remedy, but no wit sharper than the evil it cures" (*CD*, ch. vii, 168–69). Apart from this one extraordinary lapse from critical judiciousness, Gissing's social analysis of the Dickens novels seems impressively perceptive. Above all, he knows that novelists cannot simply photograph surrounding social life but must depict it through a literary medium, such as realism, satire, comedy, or romance.

In discussing Sairey Gamp of *Martin Chuzzlewit*, Gissing illuminates remarkably well the problematic relationship between literature and social reality. First he notes the sociological facts concerning this comic character. She occupies "a filthy room" in London's Holborn district sometime around 1844. This "sluttish, drunken, avaricious, dishonest woman" epitomizes nursing's debased state during that period, when even wealthy patients had to endure appallingly incompetent nurses (*CD*, ch. v, 101–2). Yet Dickens keeps Sairey amusing by a tactful censorship of disgusting details—a process that Gissing calls "delicate idealism" (*CD*, ch. v, 103–4). Most notably, her degraded London speech undergoes a selective transformation into protean verbal comedy: "this thick, gurgling flux of talk" (*CS*, "*Martin Chuzzlewit*," 81). But having long ago rejected his own earlier "idealism" as "poor" literary "stuff," Gissing distinguishes between the tactfully idealized Mrs. Gamp and the crude idealization that weakens some of Dickens's pages.[6] Although the novelist "has done his own Bowdlerizing" of Sairey Gamp by suppressing unpleasant details, he has kept her essential vulgarity (*CD*, ch. v, 103–4). But in idealizing, for example, Alice Marlow of *Dombey and Son*, Dickens substitutes false details for true ones and makes her declaim like a heroine in a stage melodrama: here, Gissing concludes, "the fact is not exalted; it has simply vanished" (*CD*, ch. v, 105).

The discussion of idealism leads Gissing into numerous perceptive comments about the effect of Dickens's novels upon Victorian England. The critic notes that their attitudes coincided with child-labor laws and other benevolent reforms. But Gissing insists that the influence between the novels and society flowed in two directions. With few exceptions, Dickens shared his readers' middle-class attitudes. In any case, he preached only those measures that he felt acceptable to his readers. He could not conceive of fiction as an assault upon the audience's basic values, and he felt deep distress whenever his works slipped in popularity. Above all, he upheld Victorian prudery and sexual hypocrisy, for "he never desired freedom to offend his public" (*CD*, ch. iv, 74–75). Gissing underscores Dickens's circumspection by comparing him with Dostoevski. In *Crime and Punishment* (1866) the great Russian novelist includes unrespectable details about his prostitute-heroine, and he makes his murderer-hero an intelligent and even visionary nihilist whose "motives" and "reasonings . . . could not be comprehended by an Englishman of the lower middle class" (*CD*, ch xi,

270). The sharp contrast between the two writers reflects the different societies in which they wrote and lived.

Gissing's broad and tolerant perspective allows him to analyze Dickens's strengths and weaknesses without patronizing that archetypal Victorian. Like Hippolyte Taine (1828–1893) and Walter Pater (1839–1894), Gissing as a critic utilizes cultural and historical relativism: "to be antiquated," he declares, "is not necessarily to be condemned, in art or anything else (save weapons of slaughter) . . ." (*CD*, ch. iv, 70). Unlike, for example, a doctrinaire Marxist, Gissing refuses to judge Dickens from a perspective that claims to correct the distorting limitations of both class and history. Thus, Gissing insists upon the equal relativity of literary gloom and Dickensian hopefulness: "Dickens has just as much right to his optimism in the world of art, as Balzac to his bitter smile" (*CD*, ch. xi, 262). In place of Balzac's saturnine humor, Gissing might well have mentioned his own. His ability to correct for both personal and cultural bias gives enduring value to his critical writings on Dickens.

By the Ionian Sea

By the Ionian Sea (written 1899; pub. 1901) transcends the limitations of a mere travel book. Gissing converts the details of his four-week Italian trip to Paola, Cosenza, Taranto, Cotrone, Catanzaro, Squillace, and Reggio into an intense evocation of a rare private experience.[7] The book describes movingly how the author's love of classical Greece and Rome transformed an often-squalid southern Italian tour into an almost-sacred pilgrimage. Still more touchingly, *By the Ionian Sea* recounts Gissing's remarkable success at making human contact with the region's living people—a contact denied to most tourists abroad by their insulated itineraries and their ignorance of any language but their own. And Gissing's closest contacts with southern Italy's people came from sharing the poignant hardships of their unclassical and often poverty-stricken environment.

A recent sociological study has noted that most tourists abroad visit only attractions selected for them by standardized guidebooks—in Paris, for instance, Notre Dame, the Eiffel Tower, and the Louvre.[8] Gissing, on the other hand, remained an inner-directed traveler. He did take along two conventional guidebooks—an English Murray's and a German Baedeker—but both works on this little-traveled region had become hopelessly outdated. He learned, for example, that an inn recommended by one of his books had degenerated long since into "a squalid and comfortless hole."[9] At Metaponto he found that the tourist "vehicle" mentioned in his guidebook had ceased to exist simply because "it did not pay . . . ; a stranger asked for it only 'once in a hundred years' " (ch. vi, 70). In fact, Gissing's original decision to tour southern Italy had come in the face of warnings from middle-class Neapolitans that sightseers never visited such a "pestilential" zone (ch. i, 3–4).

Gissing delights in uncovering a forgotten classical past beneath the concealing filth of debased southern towns—a past invisible to scattered fellow travelers, to the itinerant salesmen who find "no compensation" at all "for the miseries of" their journey "below Naples" (ch. iv, 42). In hunting for Roman and Greek traces, Gissing relies less on guidebooks than on an archaeological tome by François Lenormant—*La Grande-Grèce: paysage et histoire* [Greater Greece: Landscape and History (1881)]. This French antiquarian's account of southern Italy's ruins also describes the history surrounding them (ch. iv, 43). And Gissing himself carries his own inner map of the glory that was Greece, the grandeur that was Rome: a map derived from his classical reading. At one point, for example, he visits a thin dried-up river, the Galeso, but lovingly remembers Horace's eloquent praise of its now-vanished beauty: "*dulce* ... *Galæsi flumen*," the sweet river of Galeso (ch. v, 56–58).[10] Gissing's fond recollections of Greek and Latin writers offer valuable clues for interpreting the decayed southern landscape. The resulting juxtaposition of pathetic modern squalor and vanished ancient greatness expresses itself in elegiac lyricism—"From the eminence where I stood, how many a friend and foe of Croton has looked down upon its shining ways . . . !" (ch. vii, 85)—interspersed with rueful comedy.

Gissing's personal encounters with the people of the South provide the book's most touching moments. His fluent Italian easily surmounts the usual language barrier. In addition, his solitary state and his unglamorous route make him seem different from other tourists. Italians mistake him for "a trader of some sort," a commercial "speculator," or even a professional "architect" (ch. ii, 14–15; ch. iii, 25; ch. vii, 85; ch. viii, 97–98). Gissing easily befriends an actual traveling salesman and also enjoys sympathetic talks with a plowman, a cemetery custodian, a pair of railway workers, a schoolboy, and a priest (ch. iv, 42, 47–48; ch. viii, 95–97; ch. xvii, 215–21). Without the writer-traveler's command of the spoken vernacular, such human contacts would have remained closed off. Ironically, his Italian also allows him to make friends with Catanzaro's English Vice-Consul (ch xii, 154–58)—Great Britain's local representative, who, as the *Diary* notes, could not "speak a word of English."[11]

The sociological study of tourism mentioned above stresses a far more basic obstacle than mere ignorance of foreign languages: an almost inherent isolation of the itinerant sightseer from the "real life" that he seeks to visit. The sociologist uses the term *back region* for the site of authentic day-to-day living—a site generally closed to tourists. Thus, a sightseer may examine woven native goods in a marketplace *front* but not the grim sweatshop where the peasants do the weaving. And even the tourist who attempts penetration into the *back region* often finds no more than a mere "*stage setting*"—for example, a model factory built simply to accommodate himself and other sightseers.[12] From this sociological viewpoint, *tourist* becomes virtually synonymous with *frustrated outsider*, an outsider cut off almost inevitably from the forms of ordinary life. But Gissing the tourist overcomes this isolation partly by avoiding standard attractions but also by chance occurrences that weaken the usual barriers.

The writer-traveler's most poignant breakthrough into southern Italian life comes from a nearly fatal illness at Cotrone. When he develops fever in this pestilential town, he has to request a physician from the landlady of his shabby little inn. One Dr. Sculco arrives and diagnoses Gissing's illness as lung congestion, although the doctor behaves reassuringly. But Gissing later learns that even this kindly physician had little hope at first for his patient's recovery. In the eyes of others, Gissing changes from a mere paying guest to a fellow human threatened by a common mortal fate. As a result, the inn's vulgar-mannered hostess and her staff reveal a hidden decency. The unhygienic but pitying landlady, the polite male "chambermaid," and the numerous other servants visit the sickroom. A newsboy brings a paper every day to cheer up poor Gissing. The boy reveals that, sooner or later, everyone catches fever at Cotrone, and ultimately he himself falls ill, but after missing several days, he returns again with his papers to commiserate with Gissing over a now-shared wretchedness (ch. ix, 107–13; ch. x, 121–22, 124–28; ch. xi, 141). Above all, the writer-traveler grows attached to "my friend the doctor" (chapter nine's title). This sympathetic physician feels "amused" when his patient later describes De Quincey-like fever-dreams of Cotrone's ancient life during the second Punic War. Dr. Sculco perceptively labels them "*visioni*," "visions," for he understands that Gissing regards the classical past with an almost religious awe (ch. ix, 114–17).

In this lyrical memoir, Gissing transforms his actual travel experiences into literary art. He converts the *Diary* notes made during the trip into highly effective narrative prose. Consider below, first, a *Diary* entry about a servant who visited Gissing's sickroom and then, second, a corresponding but richer passage from *By the Ionian Sea*:

> ...The servant—a middle-aged woman, stout and very black-eyed, a pure savage—came to tell me in her terrible dialect all about the *guài* [unpleasant occurrences]—lamenting that she should be so used after having *tanto lavorato* [worked so much], and saying that her relatives were all *freddi morti* [stone dead]. I thought at first she was railing at *me*, for giving trouble, but saw her drift at last. (*Diary*, 1 December 1897, 464)

Little by little, by dint of questioning, I got what she meant. There had been *guai*, worse than usual; the mistress had reviled her unendurably for some fault or other, and was it not hard that she should be used like this after *tanto, tanto lavorato*! In fact, she was appealing for my sympathy, not abusing me at all. When she went on to say that she was alone in the world, that all her kith and kin were *freddi morti* (stone dead), a pathos in her aspect and her words took hold upon me; it was much as if some heavy-laden beast of burden had suddenly found tongue, and protested in the rude beginnings of articulate utterance against its hard lot. . . . In some measure my efforts at kindly speech succeeded, and her "Ah, Cristo!" as she turned to go away, was not without a touch of solace. (*By the Ionian Sea*, ch. x, 123–24)

If the brief *Diary* entry gives an unemotional account of a peasant woman's grumblings, the expanded version reveals how the writer's narrative skill can enrich a scene's human significance. Instead of simply listening to the complaining drudge, the sick man draws her out. After understanding her appeal for "sympathy," Gissing responds with pity, especially over her graphic lament that "all her kith and kin" are now "stone dead." Though he compares her to a talking "beast of burden," he offers the woman genuine "solace." Unlike most travel books, *By the Ionian Sea* stresses those moments when the tourist attains comradeship with others, even across the barriers of language, culture, and class.

The Private Papers of Henry Ryecroft

The Private Papers of Henry Ryecroft (1903) stands as Gissing's most cunningly appealing portrayal of the *dolce far niente*, the sweet escape from work.[13] Unlike the retired Everard Barfoot of *The Odd Women*, Ryecroft gains our essential sympathy. Gissing wins indulgence for his book-loving hermit by narrative tact and also by eloquent prose. Neither a novel nor an autobiographical memoir, *Ryecroft* takes the form of an imaginary protagonist's journal, in somewhat the same genre as Carlyle's *Sartor Resartus* (1833–1834). *Ryecroft* also has much in common with Charles Lamb's use of a literary persona in his "Essays of Elia" (1820–1826).[14] Although the *Ryecroft* papers adapt meditative passages from Gissing's own "Commonplace" and "Memorandum" books and also refer to an actual old friend—the letter-writing German E[duard]. B[ertz].—Ryecroft becomes a literary creation quite apart from his creator.[15] Professor Coustillas's annotated *Ryecroft* shows, specifically, how Gissing's extensive changes from his first to his second draft consistently work to sweeten his protagonist's character.

The fictitious biographic "Preface" by "G. G." serves to distance Gissing from the already dead Ryecroft—the imaginary author of this supposedly posthumous book.[16] As one point of contrast, their literary careers differ quite sharply. Like Alfred Yule of *New Grub Street*, Ryecroft has produced miscellaneous "hack-work": reviews, translations, "articles," and nondescript books ("Preface," viii). But his creator stuck devotedly to the novel, at least till his final years, and he shied away from journalism. In addition, Gissing and his fictional character have strikingly different private lives. After the widowed Ryecroft receives an unexpected life annuity from a dead acquaintance, this unheroic protagonist leads a sexless life in Devon, accompanied only by a humble female housekeeper. His creator, however, lived on the Continent with an extralegal "wife" rather than in monkish isolation.

This fictional character's eloquent meditations reveal a more likable human being than any of Gissing's previous depictions of happy early retirement. Compared, for example, to Everard Barfoot—*The Odd Women*'s arrogant man of leisure—Ryecroft has touching humility. Thus, this semiretired writer feels absolute contentment with his £300 a year ("Preface," p. ix)—£150 less than the income that Barfoot thought a "pittance."[17] And unlike the haughty Barfoot, Ryecroft confesses that his unearned income comes from other persons' labor, from those who toil to make possible his comfortable quarterly dividends: ". . . I know very well that every drachm [an ancient Greek coin] is sweated from human pores" ("Autumn," 173). This blunt admission from a tired old hack helps disarm the reader's criticism of the character's passive ease.

Unlike Barfoot—a perpetual world traveler—Ryecroft stays home in his beloved England and enjoys simple country pleasures. He takes unhurried walks among pastures, trees, and flowers—rural delights forbidden to him in his Grub Street days. He finds consolation in owning and touching those coveted books that he could not afford when he struggled as a London writer. He finds true happiness without sexual love or even plain companionship, because he demands little from the world. He remains content in spite of his knowledge that his death cannot now lie far off.

Most significantly, however, this Grub Street veteran, unlike Everard Barfoot, does not remain completely idle. Instead, Ryecroft writes *The Private Papers of Henry Ryecroft.* He aims, in fact, to make it his best book. The preface even assures us that he would have succeeded if only he had survived to organize his fragments ("Preface," xii). He feels poignant gratitude at his long-delayed chance to write a work that pleases him, instead of having to subsist on mere hack work. With a touching humility about his own authorship, he frankly admits that "never a page of my writing deserved to live" ("Spring," 4). Ryecroft shows an equally touching modesty about his life itself: "merely tentative, a broken series of false starts and hopeless new beginnings" ("Winter," 236). His self-deprecation has far more appeal than Barfoot's complacent belief in his own egocentric self as an exemplary "modern male" (*The Odd Women*, ch. xiii, 131).

The very organization that Gissing imposes upon Ryecroft's memoirs increases our sympathy for this literary veteran. The book's four parts—"Spring," "Summer," "Autumn," and "Winter"—correspond, of course, to life's major divisions: childhood, manhood, maturity, and death-haunted age. This commonplace equation of a year with a life stresses the brevity of Ryecroft's contentment. Yet Gissing adds subtlety to this formalized arrangement by the constant juxtaposition of present impressions with vivid past memories. Daily country pleasures alternate, for example, with Ryecroft's old struggles in Grub Street. In the closing section, "Winter," his vivid recall of warm summer outings seems almost like a dying man's hallucination of his youthful days.

With a very special appropriateness in the narrative's closing passage, Gissing employs the conventional metaphor of life as a book:

How many a time, after long labour on some piece of writing, brought at length to its conclusion, have I laid down the pen with a sigh of thankfulness; the work was full of faults, but I had wrought sincerely, had done what time and circumstance and my own nature permitted. Even so may it be with me in my last hour. May I look back on life as a long task duly completed—a piece of biography; faulty enough, but good as I could make it—and, with no thought but one of contentment, welcome the repose to follow when I have breathed the word "Finis." ("Winter," 262–63)

Ryecroft's life resembles not just any book, but one hammered out under great difficulties. In addition, his existence has literally centered itself around both reading and writing. In a sense, he has lived to make a text out of life and out of other writers' similar volumes. *Ryecroft* is that text, that printed summation of all that he has done and read. He admits that neither the author's book nor his life comes anywhere near perfection, but he adds that he has done the very best that he could at both writing and living. With sadly unknowing irony, this veteran man of letters hopes that he can "look back on life," at his death, "as a long task duly completed." In fact, he never quite finishes his memoirs, his would-be literary testament. This elegiac narrative should move any reader who has ever himself tried to write a book. For once, an old cliché applies with new relevance: in *The Private Papers of Henry Roycroft*, Gissing becomes, in truth, the proverbial "writer's writer."

Chapter Ten
Conclusion

In Gissing's own time, he soon became labeled as an overly depressing writer who failed to provide enough moral uplift for late-Victorian tastes. To twentieth-century eyes, however, his early works seem marred by excessively noble aesthetes, philanthropists, and lovers. Yet late-nineteenth-century critics found too much moral downdraft even in idealized narratives such as *A Life's Morning*, *Demos*, and *Thyrza*, apparently because of Gissing's suggestions that, within a less-than-splendid world, splendid protagonists do not always triumph. When he consciously rejected idealism in *The Emancipated*, *New Grub Street*, *Born in Exile*, and other saturnine works, the critics united in warning potential readers about Gissing's books. The less he idealized, the more insistent these critical warnings became. According to a growing consensus, his novels exuded an unpleasant lugubriousness. In response to *New Grub Street*, one typical reviewer lectured the writer about his always "grim subjects," "depressing" manner, "desperate gloom of pessimism and poverty," and "hopeless unrelieved misery."[1] Many later reviewers praised, as a welcome change, one of Gissing's least worthwhile novels, *The Town Traveller*, simply because it replaced his usual low-spiritedness with relentless jocularity.[2] Yet even Gissing's least jolly books slowly attracted a small, devoted audience.

Gissing, however, repelled the majority of readers by ignoring their wish that literature provide a rosy view of the world—an updated version of high-Victorian optimism. He rejected the widespread belief that representative government would usher in Utopia. He denied that mass education could create mass enlightenment. He doubted that simple material improvements could engender the good society. He disputed the common assertion that scientific discoveries must work for human happiness. He refused to believe that businessmen could ensure world peace merely by making international profits. Above all, as a lover of both Greece and Rome and their ancient great literatures, he dissented from the notion that the past was stupid compared to the brilliant present. Gissing's books repudiated his era's lingering faith in mankind's endless progress. In return, most readers of the late-Victorian age repudiated Gissing's books.

The early twentieth century's increasing rejection of didactic idealization encouraged a perceptive minority to value Gissing's disillusioned puncturing of sentimental dreams. He appealed especially to American writers of the Lost Generation. In the late 1920s, Christopher Morley noted that Gissing's dejected works still attracted readers, and Morley concluded that the author of such fiction as *The Odd Women* remained the perfect novelist for "moments of depression." Conrad Aiken praised Gissing's short stories for their modernity, their clear-eyed refusal to make moral judgments, and their "fine gravity of spirit." Malcolm Cowley found that the sad alienation of *New Grub Street* and *Henry Ryecroft* spoke to youthful writers of the post-Great War period.[3]

By the post-World War II era, George Orwell declared Gissing one of the few English novelists capable of depicting "credible human beings" impelled by "everyday motives." Above all, Orwell admired Gissing's descriptions of the heavily respectable "lower-middle class": its "sex-starvation," "censoriousness," and overriding insistence upon cash as the badge of social acceptance. This twentieth-century critic thought it "a point in" Gissing's "favour that he had no very strong moral purpose" but wrote undidactically about sensitive people condemned to isolation by a culture's "ugliness, emptiness and cruelty." If Orwell himself dissected expanding mass culture, he considered *New Grub Street* Gissing's finest achievement—that classic account of thin-skinned authors in a world that esteems writing only for its cash value.[4] One might call Gissing Orwell's "only begetter." The intelligent and sensitive protagonists of the later writer's fiction struggle against squalid lower-middle-class environments in the true Gissing way, perhaps most characteristically in *Keep the Aspidistra Flying* (1936). Even Orwell's best-known work, *Nineteen Eighty-Four* (1949), seems full of Gissing touches, as Winston Smith trudges through an anti-utopian London of bad smells, bad plumbing, and degraded city "proles." From Gissing to George Orwell, from 1891 to 1984, the distance is far less than one might have supposed.

As the idealizing didacticism of the high-Victorian era receded into the past, late-twentieth-century critics could view with widened perspective Gissing's resistance to the art of moral uplift. Thus Jacob Korg's *George Gissing: A Critical Biography* (1963) studies the writer's output within the framework of late-Victorian culture. Korg sees Gissing's development as an ongoing struggle between contradictory tendencies: reformism versus art for art's sake. In *The Born Exile* (1974), Gillian Tindall shows that the writer's depiction of society's moral dilemmas reflects the man's private relationships. She demonstrates convincingly that Gissing often used his fiction to explore a course of action before carrying it out; thus, *Denzil Quarrier*'s pretended marriage foreshadows the author's own pretended marriage to Gabrielle Fleury. Adrian Poole's *Gissing in Context* (1975) relates the novelist to other major Victorians—including Hardy, Meredith, Dickens, Thackeray, and Charlotte Brontë—and explores Gissing's themes, prose style, plots, imagery, and characterization.[5]

In addition, many critics have begun to examine Gissing's representation of late-Victorian society. John Goode has written significant analyses of Gissing's imaginative reaction to English capitalism, socialism, humanitarianism, and ubiquitous urban blight. Goode focuses upon the writer's deepening gloom about the possibility of widespread reform or even of private resistance to the debasing effects of social forces and economic pressures.[6] P. J. Keating's *The Working Classes in Victorian Fiction* places Gissing among other authors who portrayed the laboring class: Dickens,

Kingsley, Gaskell, Kipling, and numerous lesser figures. Robert L. Selig has analyzed Gissing's treatment of expanding mass culture as a harmful influence upon writers and their audience. John Gross and Bernard Bergonzi have also discussed this key Gissing theme yet have warned that the novelist saw cultural alienation through a distorting personal lens.[7] Such feminist critics as Maria Teresa Chialant and Nina Auerbach have investigated Gissing's complex response to the late-Victorian "woman question." Chialant notes his class-bound exclusion of proletarian women from equality with middle-class females and with men, but Auerbach praises his sympathetic treatment of an all-female community.[8] The 1970s and 1980s saw a Gissing revival of some extent among knowledgeable readers, as even the lesser novels came back into print. The *Gissing Newsletter* has survived and prospered well into its second decade, and its editor, Pierre Coustillas, has himself encouraged new interest in the writer by a steady production of books, monographs, and essays. And in 1978 the citizens of Wakefield set up a Gissing Trust in order to preserve his birthplace as a center for study of both the man and his books.

Gissing's most substantial contributions to English fiction followed his rejection of idealism in 1888.[9] Concentrating thereafter on human disillusionment with all lofty ideals, he wrote the works that Orwell hailed as protests "against the . . . self-torture that goes by the name of respectability."[10] Gissing's studies of grubby disenchantment reflect a central tendency of nineteenth-century realism, exemplified in two memorable fictional protagonists: Flaubert's Emma in *Madame Bovary* (1856–1857), who comes to grief by confusing provincial actualities with romantic daydreams, and George Eliot's Dr. Lydgate in *Middlemarch* (1871–1872), who finds his visionary medical goals frustrated by small-town prejudices. But as George Eliot's close successor in English realism, Gissing, at least after 1888, abandoned her insistent exhortations for moral behavior even in an amoral universe. This absence of didacticism gives his major books an almost Continental flavor of tough-minded skepticism.

Gissing's finest novels depict intelligent and sensitive human beings whose constricted social sphere makes their lingering ideals not merely anachronisms, but outright hindrances. Certain distinctive lower-middle-class figures become his unique specialty: educated but moneyless males, thinking women victimized by sexual discrimination, and fastidious persons of both sexes benumbed by the spreading vulgarity of modern urban life. Gissing's two most impressive works—*New Grub Street* (1891) and *Born in Exile* (1892)—reveal, in contrasting ways, the helplessness of alienated lower-middle-class citizens to escape from society's meshes. In *New Grub Street*, the scrupulosity of Reardon and Biffen ensures their literary failure. In *Born in Exile*, Peak's dishonest attempt to marry into the gentry damages his sense of personal worth. Neither morality nor amorality can save these Gissing characters from a world of social frustrations.

In summarizing Gissing's achievement, one should stress, above all, his tenacious literary development. Through even the most squalid personal reversals, he kept on writing with a singleness of purpose, with a stubborn perseverance that belies the Gissing myth of a man defeated by gloom. In a life cut short at only forty-six, he hammered out twenty-two novels, four major works of nonfiction, and well over one hundred short stories. He ultimately achieved a solid place in English letters. More than a century after he first broke into print, Gissing's books remain very much alive.

Notes and References

Chapter One

1. Clifford Brook identifies the trade of Gissing's grandfather in "Three George Gissings," *Gissing Newsletter* 15 (January 1979):29; hereafter referred to as *GN*. Details about Thomas Gissing appear in George Gissing's "Reminscences [*sic*] of my Father jotted down from time to time as they by chance occur to me," notebook, Beinecke Rare Book and Manuscript Library, Yale University—hereafter referred to as "Reminiscences." Three of Thomas Gissing's books were [T. W. Gissing], *Margaret, and Other Poems*, by an East Anglian (London, 1855); T. W. Gissing, *The Ferns and Fern Allies of Wakefield* (Wakefield, 1862); T. W. Gissing, *Materials for a Flora of Wakefield* (London, 1867). Two unidentified other "slender volumes of verse" by Thomas Gissing are mentioned by Pierre Coustillas, ed., "Who's Who in Gissing's Diary," *London and the Life of Literature in Late Victorian England: The Diary of George Gissing, Novelist* (Lewisburg, Pa., 1978), p. 576, hereafter referred to as *Diary*.

2. George Gissing, "Dickens in Memory," *Critical Studies of the Works of Charles Dickens* (New York, 1965), p. 154. The essay was written in 1901.

3. "Reminiscences." For Mrs. Gissing's churchgoing, see Clifford Brook, "The Baptism Records of George Gissing and His Brothers and Sisters," *GN* 13 (January 1977):17–19. The profession of Mrs. Gissing's father is mentioned by John Spiers and Pierre Coustillas, *The Rediscovery of George Gissing: A Reader's Guide* (London, 1971), p. 16.

4. "Reminiscences."

5. Pierre Coustillas, comp., with the assistance of Clifford Brook, "Recollections of Margaret and Ellen Gissing," *GN* 12 (January 1976):5, 10, 11.

6. Letter of George Gissing to Algernon Gissing, 19 June 1881, Beinecke.

7. For Gissing's early schooling and his attitude toward his father, see Jacob Korg, *George Gissing: A Critical Biography* (Seattle, 1963), p. 8—hereafter referred to as Korg, *GG*; Letter of George Gissing to his son Walter Gissing, 2 October 1896, Beinecke; "Reminiscences." For Gissing's schooling at Lindow Grove, see Pierre Coustillas, "Henry Hick's Recollections of George Gissing," *Huntington Library Quarterly* 29 (February 1966): 166; George Gissing, "The Old School," *Dinglewood Magazine*, December 1897, pp. 2–4, reprinted and introduced by P[ierre]. Coustillas in "George Gissing à Alderley Edge," *Études Anglaises* 20 (April-June 1967): 174–78; George Gissing: a collection of 14 of his school and university certificates, 1869–75, Beinecke. For Thomas Gissing's oral readings, see "Reminiscences." Until 1978, scholars believed that Gissing ranked first in all of England in the Oxford Local Examination. In fact, he ranked twelfth. On this point, see P[ierre]. Coustillas, "Gissing's Academic Feat Reconsidered," *GN* 15 (October 1979): 12–15.

8. For Gissing's unusual arrangement at Lindow Grove, see Spiers and Coustillas, *Rediscovery*, p. 21; [Pierre Coustillas], "Editor's Note" to Francis Noel Lees's "George Gissing at College," *GN* 5 (April 1969): 11. For his college honors, see *Rediscovery*, p. 21; school and university certificates, Beinecke. For the B.A. examinations required in the 1870s, see Joseph Thompson, *The Owens College: Its Foundation and Growth; and Its Connection with the Victoria University, Manchester* (Manchester: J. E. Cornish, 1886), pp. 206–7.

9. Spiers and Coustillas, *Rediscovery*, p. 21; Edward Fiddes, *Chapters in the History of Owens College and of Manchester University, 1851–1914* (Manchester: Manchester University Press, 1937), pp. 116–17. P[ierre]. Coustillas, "George Gissing à Manchester," *Études Anglaises* 16 (July-September 1963): 256n.; Seventeen letters of George Gissing to his school friend at Lindow Grove, Arthur Bowes, Beinecke.

10. Coustillas, "Gissing à Manchester," pp. 255–61.

11. Fiddes, *Chapters*, pp. 26–27, 54.

12. Coustillas, "Gissing à Manchester," pp. 255–61; Korg, *GG*, pp. 11–13.

13. "Margaret," in *Margaret, and Other Poems*, p. 11.

14. *Margaret*, pp. 19–24.

15. *Diary*, p. 23.

16. "A Farewell," a poem in Gissing's notebook of unpublished poems, 1869–1882, Beinecke.

17. [George Gissing], "Art Notes." "'Elaine'—Rosenthal and Tojetti," *Commonwealth*, 28 October 1876, identified in Spiers and Coustillas, *Rediscovery*, p. 24. For Dr. Zakrzewska, see Coustillas, "Who's Who in Gissing's Diary," p. 590. For comments on Garrison and the *Atlantic*, see Letter of George Gissing to his brother William Gissing, 5 October 1876, *Letters of George Gissing to Members of His Family*, collected and arranged by Algernon and Ellen Gissing, with a preface by his son (London, 1927), p. 14.

18. *Letters to Family*, pp. 19–21.

19. Korg, *GG*, pp. 6–7, 16.

20. Ibid., pp. 17–18; George Gissing, "The Sins of the Fathers," in *Sins of the Fathers and Other Tales*, with an Introduction by Vincent Starrett (Chicago, 1924), pp. 1–31; Pierre Coustillas and Robert L. Selig, "Unknown Gissing Stories from Chicago," *Times Literary Supplement* (London), 12 December 1980, pp. 1417–18; *Letters to Family*, pp. 57–58.

21. Korg, *GG*, pp. 18–20; Mabel Collins Donnelly, *George Gissing: Grave Comedian* (Cambridge, Mass., 1954), pp. 29–33.

22. Although Gissing did not marry Nell until two years later when he felt more confident of succeeding as a writer, Algernon and Ellen Gissing's white lie that George actually married his future wife by the fall of 1877 seems pointless unless the lovers were living together by then (*Letters to Family*, p. 22).

23. Korg, *GG*, pp. 21–22; Spiers and Coustillas, *Rediscovery*, p. 31; *Letters to Family*, pp. 26, 30, 32, 34, 39.

24. Korg, *GG*, p. 25.

25. Ibid., p. 26.

26. Gissing married Nell on 27 October 1879 in the Parish Church of St. James, Hampstead Road (Spiers and Coustillas, *Rediscovery*, pp. 25–26). He completed *Workers*, except for revisions, on 13 November 1879 (*Letters to Family*, p. 49). On this odd chronological sequence, see Gillian Tindall, *The Born Exile: George Gissing* (London, 1974), pp. 80–83. For the suggestion that Gissing added Carrie as a character in *Workers* only after he had married Nell, see Michael Collie, *The Alien Art: A Critical Study of George Gissing's Novels* (Folkestone, Kent, 1979), pp. 35–41.

27. Korg, *GG*, pp. 48–51, 58–59. George describes the hidden gin bottle in a letter to Algernon Gissing, 18 January 1882, Beinecke.

28. Korg, *GG*, pp. 3–6, 23–24, 32, 44–48, 50–51, 53–54; *Letters to Family*, pp. 56–58; Spiers and Coustillas, *Rediscovery*, p. 42. For an account of "Mrs. Grundy's Enemies," see Royal A. Gettmann, *A Victorian Publisher: A Study of the Bentley Papers* (Cambridge, 1960), pp. 215–22.

29. For Gissing's well-to-do employers, see Donnelly, *Gissing*, pp. 77–79, and Korg, *GG*, pp. 45, 69–70. For Gissing's humble meal, see Letter of George Gissing to Margaret Gissing, 12 July 1882, Henry W. and Albert A. Berg Collection of the New York Public Library, Astor, Lenox and Tilden Foundations. For the conversation about butlers, see Korg, *GG*, p. 45. For Gissing's new quarters at 7K Cornwall Residences near Baker Street Station, see Korg, *GG*, pp. 73–74.

30. Letter of George Gissing to Ellen Gissing, 14 March 1886, Berg.

31. *Letters to Family*, p. 172.

32. *Diary*, pp. 21–22, 27–28.

33. Letter of George Gissing to Ellen Gissing, 20 October 1889, *Letters to Family*, p. 290.

34. For details of this trip, see *Diary*, pp. 58–142.

35. *Diary*, pp. 144–68.

36. Ibid., pp. 153, 155–56, 159, 166–67, 169–70. Miss Sichel's signed article was entitled "Two Philanthropic Novelists: Mr. Walter Besant and Mr. George Gissing," *Murray's Magazine* 3 (April 1888): 506–18.

37. *The Letters of George Gissing to Eduard Bertz, 1887–1903*, ed. Arthur C. Young (New Brunswick, N.J., 1961), pp. 76–78; Letter of George Gissing to Edith Sichel, 15 October 1889, Berg.

38. *Diary*, pp. 171, 175, 181.

39. Ibid., pp. 189, 195.

40. Letter of George Gissing to Ellen Gissing, 7 October 1890, Berg; *Diary*, pp. 206–10.

41. For Gissing's pattern of work and frustration, see *Diary*, pp. 210–22. For the Connie Ash affair, see *Diary*, pp. 223–24. Gissing's hopes about Miss Ash appear in his letter to Ellen Gissing, 12 August 1890, Berg. For his sales and earnings to this time, see Spiers and Coustillas, *Rediscovery*, pp. 60, 62, 66, 70. For his resolve to find a working girl, see *Letters to Bertz*, p. 110.

42. For the sources of the first three theories about the place, see Young, "Introduction," *Letters to Bertz*, p. xxx. The music-hall meeting place is suggested by the entry of 24 September 1890, *Diary*, p. 226, and by Coustillas's note, p. 555. The Kew meeting place comes from a Letter of George Gissing to Ellen Gissing, 7 October 1890, Berg.

43. *Diary*, pp. 224–27.

44. Gordon S. Haight, "Gissing: Some Biographical Details," *Notes and Queries*, o.s. 209, n.s. 11 (June 1964):235–36; Pierre Coustillas, "Gissing: Some More Biographical Details," *Notes and Queries*, o.s. 211, n.s. 13 (February 1966):68–69; Letter of George Gissing, 7 October 1890, Berg.

45. *Letters to Bertz*, pp. 110, 115–16; *Diary*, pp. 227–36.

46. *Diary*, pp. 228–31, 235–37; Letter of George Gissing to Ellen Gissing, 20 January 1891, Berg.

47. *Diary*, pp. 238–40.

48. Ibid., pp. 245, 247, 262–63, 265, 267, 276–80, 286–87, 291–93, 295–96, 304, 317, 323, 326, 348, 350, 371, 374–77, 379, 385–88, 395–97, 401–5, 407–8, 413–15, 418, 424–27, 430, 435, 438–45, 446–90; Korg, *GG*, pp. 223–24.

49. *Diary*, pp. 499–501; Korg, *GG*, pp. 224, 226.

50. Letter of George Gissing to Algernon Gissing, 26 January 1902, Beinecke; *Letters to Bertz*, pp. 305–6; Coustillas, "Who's Who in Gissing's Diary," p. 576.

51. For Gissing's growing reputation, see *Diary*, pp. 285, 309, 340, 360, 362, 421; Korg, *GG*, pp. 202–3; Spiers and Coustillas, *Rediscovery*, p. 110.

52. On the sale of Gissing's books, the market for his short stories, and his income from this period, see Korg, *GG*, p. 167; Spiers and Coustillas, *Rediscovery*, pp. 55, 76, 83, 89, 94–96, 110.

53. For some of Gissing's literary friends, see *Diary*, pp. 311, 385, 387–88, 413, 427, 429. For Bullen's comment, see *Diary*, pp. 296–97. For some of the women who approached Gissing, see *Diary*, pp. 304–6, 310, 315, 364–67, 372, 378, 395, 399, 414.

54. For Gissing's wish for a divorce, see *Diary*, p. 509, and *The Letters of George Gissing to Gabrielle Fleury*, ed. Pierre Coustillas (New York, 1964), pp. 43–44, 103, 105. For Gissing's association of courtship with literary fame, see *Letters to Fleury*, pp. 29, 51. For

his first meeting with Gabrielle, see *Diary*, pp. 496–97. For his sentimental courtship, see almost any page of *Letters to Fleury* from pp. 27–130.

55. Coustillas, "Introduction," *Letters to Fleury*, pp. 10–12; Korg, *GG*, pp. 228–29; *Letters to Bertz*, pp. 253–54. H. G. Wells's contrasting denigration of Gabrielle may have resulted from his own insensitive chauvinism. See H. G. Wells, *Experiment in Autobiography* (London, 1934), 2:576–81, and Royal A. Gettmann, ed., *George Gissing and H. G. Wells: Their Friendship and Correspondence* (Urbana, Ill., 1961), p. 110n.

56. "Henry Hick's Recollections," p. 167; "Introduction," *Letters to Fleury*, pp. 14–19; *Letters to Bertz*, p. 257; Gettmann, *Gissing and Wells*, pp. 135, 163, 184.

57. Gettmann, *Gissing and Wells*, pp. 153, 160–91; *Letters to Bertz*, pp. 295–98, 306, 323–24; *Letters to Fleury*, pp. 133–66; Korg, *GG*, pp. 250–52.

Chapter Two

1. George Gissing, *Charles Dickens: A Critical Study* (St. Clair Shores, Mich., 1976), ch. x, p. 243; the first edition was that of London, 1898. Because no standard collected edition of Gissing's works exists, I shall give chapter and page number in referring to each book and, when necessary, shall also provide volume and part number.

2. P. J. Keating, *The Working Classes in Victorian Fiction* (London, 1971), pp. 5, 20, 46, 68–69.

3. Quoted by Richard Stang in *The Theory of the Novel in England, 1850–1870* (New York: Columbia University Press, 1959), p. 155.

4. Gettmann, *Victorian Publisher*, pp. 215–22.

5. Louis Cazamian, *The Social Novel in England 1830–1850: Dickens, Disraeli, Mrs. Gaskell, Kingsley*, tr. Martin Fido (London: Routledge & Kegan Paul, 1973), pp. 117–47.

6. See above, "Preface."

7. George Gissing, *Workers in the Dawn*, ed. Robert Shafer (Garden City, N.Y., 1935); hereafter referred to in the text by volume, part, chapter, and page number.

8. Tindall, *Born Exile*, p. 84. For convincing evidence that the introduction of Carrie Mitchell as Arthur's prostitute wife came as a

late afterthought in the writing of the novel, see Collie, *Alien Art*, pp. 35–40.

9. Erich Auerbach, *Mimesis: The Representation of Reality in Western Literature*, tr. Willard Trask (Garden City, N.Y.: Doubleday Anchor Books, 1957), p. 489.

10. George Gissing, "Preface to the New Edition," *The Unclassed* (London, 1901); hereafter referred to in the text by chapter and page number. This 1901 edition reprints Gissing's 1895 revision of *The Unclassed*—far superior artistically to the original 1884 edition.

11. *Charles Dickens: A Critical Study*, ch. vii, pp. 168–69.

12. On *Demos*'s fortuitous success, see Spiers and Coustillas, *Rediscovery*, pp. 50–55.

13. For detailed discussions of *Demos*, see John Goode, "Gissing, Morris and English Socialism," *Victorian Studies* 12 (December 1968):201–26; Alan Lelchuk, "*Demos*: The Ordeal of the Two Gissings," *Victorian Studies* 12 (March 1969):357–74; John Goode and Alan Lelchuk, "Gissing's *Demos*: A Controversy," *Victorian Studies* 12 (June 1969):431–40.

14. George Gissing, *Demos: A Story of English Socialism* (New York, [1928]), ch. iv, p. 33; hereafter referred to in the text by chapter and page number.

15. E. J. Hobsbawm, "The Labour Aristocracy in Nineteenth-Century Britain," in *Labouring Men: Studies in the History of Labour* (New York: Basic Books, 1964), pp. 272–75, 312–13.

16. For Gissing's indebtedness to Milliken's cartoons, see Keating, *Working Classes*, pp. 140, 154–55.

17. George Gissing, *Thyrza: A Tale* (New York, [1928]), ch. xxxiii, p. 399; hereafter referred to in the text by chapter and page number. This 1928 text reprints Gissing's 1891 one-volume revision of *Thyrza*—a considerable improvement over the original digressive three-decker. But *Thyrza*'s first edition (London, 1887) contains one particularly revealing digression that Gissing later omitted: the unrequited love of the married Harold Emerson, a talentless poet, for the virtuous heroine. This farcical episode serves as a self-exploding device that mocks the novel's own principal love story.

18. Tindall, *Born Exile*, pp. 89–97.

19. Richard Hoggart, *The Uses of Literacy: Changing Patterns in English Mass Culture* (Fair Lawn: N.J.: Essential Books, 1957), p. 129.

20. For a stimulating analysis of *The Nether World*, see John Goode, "George Gissing's *The Nether World*," in *Tradition and Tolerance in Nineteenth-Century Fiction: Critical Essays on Some English and American Novels*, by David Howard, John Lucas, and John Goode (London, 1966), pp. 207–41. See also Walter Allen, "Introduction," *The Nether World*, by George Gissing (London, 1973), pp. v–xvii. This edition of *The Nether World* shall hereafter be referred to in the text by chapter and volume number.

21. After becoming dissatisfied with his first version of this chapter, Gissing renounced his tendency toward "idealism." See above, "Preface."

Chapter Three

1. See above, Chap. 9.

2. George Gissing, *Isabel Clarendon*, ed. Pierre Coustillas (Brighton, Sussex, 1969), II, chs. iv and v; hereafter referred to in the text by volume, chapter, and page number. For a helpful discussion of the novel, see Professor Coustillas's introduction to this edition, pp. xv–lx. See also J. Middleton Murry, "George Gissing," in his *Katherine Mansfield and Other Literary Studies* (London, 1959), pp. 13–14.

3. F. M. L. Thompson, *English Landed Society in the Nineteenth Century* (London: Routledge & Kegan Paul, 1963), pp. 1–24.

4. Ibid., p. 129.

5. George Orwell, "George Gissing," in *Collected Articles on George Gissing*, ed. Pierre Coustillas (New York, 1968), p. 52.

6. George Gissing, *A Life's Morning* (New York, [1914]); hereafter referred to in the text by chapter and page number.

7. The Hood-Dagworthy-Emily plot bears a strong resemblance to the Claudio-Angelo-Isabella plot in Shakespeare's *Measure for Measure*—a resemblance noted by the narrator himself in ch. xi, p. 172, of the novel.

8. On the three generations needed for making a gentleman, see Thompson, *English Landed Society*, p. 129. On gentlemanly training and gentlemanly occupations, see the same work, pp. 16–17, 129, 131–34.

9. Morley Roberts, "Introduction," *A Life's Morning*, pp. v–viii.

10. George Gissing, *The Emancipated* (Chicago, 1895), pt. II,

ch. i, pp. 245, 248–49; hereafter referred to in the text by part, chapter, and page number.

11. A few critics have appreciated *The Emancipated*. See, for example, Korg, *GG*, pp. 136–40.

12. Sir James [Fitzjames] Stephen, Lord Selborne, the Rev. Dr. [James] Martineau, Frederic Harrison, the Dean [Richard William Church] of St. Paul's, the Duke of Argyll, Professor [William Kingdon] Clifford, Dr. [William George] Ward, Professor [Thomas Henry] Huxley, R[ichard]. H[olt]. Hutton, "A Modern Symposium. Subject: 'The Influence upon Morality of a Decline in Religious Belief,'" *Nineteenth Century* 1 (April 1877):331–58; (May 1877): 531–46.

13. For an account of the metaphysical society and its connection with the *Nineteenth Century*, see Alan Williard Brown, *The Metaphysical Society: Victorian Minds in Crisis, 1869–1886* (New York: Columbia University Press, 1947), especially p. 38 on "A Modern Symposium." For Gissing's friendships with Harrison and Morley, see above, Chap. 1.

14. Huxley, in "A Modern Symposium," p. 537.

15. Matthew Arnold, *Culture and Anarchy*, in *The Works of Matthew Arnold* (London: Macmillan & Co., Smith, Elder & Co., 1903), 6:26. The book's first edition was in 1869.

Chapter Four

1. George Gissing, *New Grub Street* (New York, 1926), ch. iv, p. 53; hereafter referred to in the text by chapter and page number.

2. An otherwise perceptive critic, John Goode, has erred in calling Jasper Milvain "sexless." See John Goode, *George Gissing: Ideology and Fiction* (New York, 1979), p. 117; hereafter referred to as Goode, *GG*.

3. For further discussions of *New Grub Street* as a study of writers' lives, see Robert L. Selig, "'The Valley of the Shadow of Books': Alienation in Gissing's *New Grub Street*," *Nineteenth-Century Fiction* 25 (September 1970):188–98; John Gross, "Introduction," *New Grub Street* (London, 1967), pp. v–xii; Irving Howe, "George Gissing: Poet of Fatigue," in his *A World More Attractive: A View of Modern Literature and Politics* (New York, 1963), pp. 169–91; Bernard Bergonzi, "The Novelist as Hero," *Twentieth Century* 164

(November 1958):444–55; Q. D. Leavis, "Gissing and the English Novel," *Scrutiny* 7 (June 1938):73–81.

4. Matthew Arnold, "Stanzas from the Grand Chartreuse," ll. 49–54, in *The Poetical Works of Matthew Arnold*, ed. C. B. Tinker and H. F. Lowry (London: Oxford University Press, 1950), pp. 300–301.

5. "Grand Chartreuse," ll. 85–86, in ibid., p. 302.

6. G[resham]. M'C[ready]. S[ykes]., "Prisons and Penology," *New Encyclopaedia Britannica: Macropaedia*, 1979 ed., 14:1099a.

7. For a useful discussion of late supplemental pages added to *Born in Exile*'s already-paginated fair-copy manuscript (a manuscript now in the Huntington Library), see Collie, *Alien Art*, pp. 142–44. He reveals that originally the work was "narrated principally from the point of view of . . . Godwin Peak," but Collie's critical praise of the interpolated shifts away from the main character seems unconvincing. Even the padding provided by these departures from Peak left the book too short to suit the publisher. In order to bring the pages to an acceptable number, Gissing had to write and insert the second-to-last chapter just before the novel went to press (*Diary*, p. 274).

8. For stimulating discussions of *Born in Exile*, see Jacob Korg, "The Spiritual Theme of George Gissing's *Born in Exile*," in *From Jane Austen to Joseph Conrad: Essays Collected in Memory of James T. Hillhouse*, ed. Robert C. Rathburn and Martin Steinmann (Minneapolis, 1958), pp. 246–56; Goode, *GG*, pp. 59–70. Gissing's interest in contemporary theories of the unconscious has considerable relevance to the novel. In 1889 he took extensive notes on Théodule Ribot's *L'Hérédité psychologique* (1873). Ribot, a professor of experimental psychology, emphasized unconscious motives in human thought and action. See *Diary*, p. 170, and *George Gissing's Commonplace Book: A Manuscript in the Berg Collection of the New York Public Library*, ed. Jacob Korg (New York, 1962), pp. 59–62.

9. George Gissing, *Born in Exile* (London, [1913]), pt. I, ch. i, p. 28; hereafter referred to in the text by part, chapter, and page number.

10. See above, note 17 for Chap. 2.

11. A distant fictional cousin of Peak, the artisan Jude Fawley in Thomas Hardy's *Jude the Obscure* (1896), furnishes a rustic equivalent of Peak's alienation. Jude yearns to gain admission to college but cannot.

12. Hoggart, *The Uses of Literary*, pp. 238–49.

13. For *Born in Exile*'s references to Peak's self-conscious stiffness, see pt. I, ch. iii, 58, 77–78; pt. I, ch. v, 102–3; pt. II, ch. iv, 179. For his resentful and harsh gracelessness, see pt. III, ch. v, 293–94; pt. V, ch. iv, 437.

Chapter Five

1. H. G. Wells, "The Novels of Mr. George Gissing," in *George Gissing and H. G. Wells*, pp. 251; reprinted from *Contemporary Review* 72 (August 1897):192–201.

2. See, for example, Maria Teresa Chialant, "*The Odd Women* di George Gissing, e il movimento femminista" [George Gissing's *The Odd Women* and the Feminist Movement], *Annali Istituto Universitario Orientale, Napoli, Sezione Germanica* 10 (1967):155–87; Nina Auerbach, *Communities of Women: An Idea in Fiction* (Cambridge, Mass., 1978), pp. 141–57.

3. George Gissing, *The Odd Women* (New York, 1971), ch. xiv, p. 145; hereafter referred to in the text by chapter and page number.

4. Gissing modeled his feminist school on Emilia Jessie Boucherett's Society for Promoting the Employment of Women, founded in 1859 but still active in the 1890s (Joyce Evans, "Some Notes on *The Odd Women* and the Woman's Movement," *GN* 2 [September 1966]:1–4). For opinions strikingly like those of Mary Barfoot, see [Emilia Jessie] Boucherett, [An untitled address on The Society for Promoting the Employment of Women], *English Woman's Journal* 5 (1 August 1860):393–94.

5. On the Victorian gospel of work, see Walter E. Houghton, *The Victorian Frame of Mind, 1830–1870* (New Haven: Yale University Press, 1957), pp. 242–62.

6. Ibid., p. 245.

7. Robert L. Selig, "The Gospel of Work in *The Odd Women*: Gissing's Double Standard," *Supplement* to *GN* 15 (January 1979): 20.

8. Walter Allen, *The English Novel: A Short Critical History* (New York, 1958), p. 349.

9. *Letters to Bertz*, p. 193.

10. In a suppressed portion of the manuscript to which Gissing's

publisher objected, Nancy forces Tarrant into marriage by threatening to sue for breach of promise. See Collie, *Alien Art*, pp. 156–57. Yet even with the inclusion of this episode, Tarrant's later behavior toward Nancy would still seem unjustifiably callous.

11. George Gissing, *In the Year of Jubilee* (London, 1894), III, pt. V, ch. v, pp. 97, 99; hereafter referred to in the text by volume, part, chapter, and page.

12. For a discussion of *Jubilee* as a study of the inherent frustrations of suburbia, see Goode, *GG*, pp. 163–80.

13. For an illuminating discussion of the upgrading of taste by the mass media, see Daniel Bell, "Modernity and Mass Society: On the Varieties of Cultural Experience," *Studies in Public Communication*, no. 4 (Autumn 1962):8.

14. For a detailed discussion of advertising and popular songs in the novel, see Robert L. Selig, "A Sad Heart at the Late-Victorian Culture Market: George Gissing's *In the Year of Jubilee*," *Studies in English Literature* 9 (Autumn 1969):703–20.

15. On recurring British financial crises in this period, see R. C. K. Ensor, *England 1870–1914* (Oxford: Clarendon Press, 1936), pp. 111–12, 282–83.

16. This Coventry bicycle investment in the fictional year of 1888 reflects actuality: J. K. Starley developed the first safety bicycle at Coventry in 1885, and J. B. Dunlop patented the pneumatic bicycle tire in 1888 (Ensor, *England 1870–1914*, p. 338).

17. On this point, see ibid., pp. 112–14.

18. On the Victorian ideal of home, see Houghton, *Victorian Frame of Mind*, pp. 341–48.

19. George Gissing, *The Whirlpool* (New York, 1897), pt. III, ch. i, p. 304.

Chapter Six

1. For the fullest account of Mudie's and the three-volume novel, see Guinevere L. Griest, *Mudie's Circulating Library and the Victorian Novel* (Bloomington: Indiana University Press, 1970).

2. Ibid., pp. 171–75.

3. On this point, see ibid., pp. 48–49.

4. Gissing wrote *Denzil Quarrier* from 6 October to 12 November 1891 (*Diary*, pp. 257–60). His search for a publisher of *Born in Exile*

lasted from 20 July to 29 December 1891 (*Diary*, pp. 251–65). In fact, *Denzil Quarrier* was published before *Born in Exile*.

5. See above, Chap. 1.

6. This situation seems almost a travesty of Henrik Ibsen's *Rosmersholm* (1886), which Gissing had read with some puzzlement: "In evening read 'Rosmersholm,' a strange piece, which I don't quite understand" (*Diary*, 10 June 1888, p. 31).

7. E. M. Forster, *Aspects of the Novel* (New York: Harcourt, Brace, 1927), pp. 135–36. Among Trollope's finest political novels are *Phineas Finn, the Irish Member* (1867–1869), *Phineas Redux* (1873–1874), and *The Prime Minister* (1875–1876).

8. See Ensor, *England 1870–1914*, pp. 62–63.

9. George Gissing, *Denzil Quarrier* (New York, 1892), ch. iii, pp. 25–26; ch. xv, p. 162; hereafter referred to in the text by chapter and page number.

10. Significantly, Quarrier actually does write a book (*Denzil Quarrier*, ch. xxvi, p. 298).

11. Gissing read Henrik Ibsen's *Pillars of Society* (1877) on 10 June 1888 (*Diary*, p. 31).

12. If we count false starts, *Eve's Ransom* itself took Gissing eighty-four days (*Diary*, 17 April to 29 June 1894, pp. 335–40). For the *Diary*'s record of Gissing's struggles with "The Iron Gods," see 20 December 1892 to 22 April 1893, pp. 292–302, and also the discouraged later comment of 1 August 1893, p. 311: "Grew sick of my Birmingham story. Doubt whether I shall go on with it." No manuscript of "The Iron Gods" survives.

13. George Gissing, *Eve's Ransom* (New York, 1895), ch. xxvii, p. 376; hereafter referred to in the text by chapter and page number.

14. *Letters to Bertz*, 2 December 1892, p. 163; see also Gissing's letter to his brother Algernon, 28 February 1893, *Letters to Family*, p. 332.

15. *Letters to Bertz*, 2 December 1892, p. 163; *Diary*, 3–24 November 1892, pp. 288–90.

16. T. H. Marshall, "The Recent History of Professionalism in Relation to Social Structure and Social Policy," in *Class, Citizenship, and Social Development* (Garden City, N.Y.: Doubleday, 1964), pp. 144–46.

17. *Letters to Bertz*, 18 December 1895, p. 209. Gissing wrote *Sleeping Fires* from 15 January to 1 March 1895 (*Diary*, pp. 360–65).

18. George Gissing, *Sleeping Fires* (New York, 1896), ch. i, p. 3; hereafter referred to in the text by chapter and page number.

19. Letter of George Gissing to Morley Roberts, 10 February 1895, quoted in Morley Roberts, "The Letters of George Gissing," *Virginia Quarterly Review* 7 (July 1931):418.

20. An 1895 entry records how Gissing combed his diary's earlier pages as a preparation for writing *Sleeping Fires* (*Diary*, 14 January 1895, p. 360). For Gissing's trip to Greece, see *Diary*, 19 November to 18 December 1889, pp. 174–92.

21. Gissing's *Diary* entry for 21 November 1889, on p. 176, describes this dusting of hotel customers as the usual procedure of Athenian waiters.

22. *Diary*, 22 April to 16 July 1895, pp. 371–80.

23. George Gissing, *The Paying Guest* (New York, 1895), ch. i, p. 29; hereafter referred to in the text by chapter and page number.

24. Letter of George Gissing to Morley Roberts, 10 February 1895, quoted in "The Letters of George Gissing," p. 417.

25. "Henry Hick's Recollections," p. 169.

26. *Diary*, 28 April 1895, p. 372.

Chapter Seven

1. See above, Chap. 1.

2. See above, Chap. 6.

3. Gissing's laborious efforts to write *The Town Traveller* stretched from 1 February to 14 July 1897 (*Diary*, pp. 434–38). His immersion in Dickens for a critical study took up much of 1897 (*Diary*, pp. 435–53). Gissing first met Wells on 20 November 1896 (*Diary*, p. 427).

4. H. G. Wells, *The Wheels of Chance* (New York: Macmillan, 1896), ch. x, p. 69. The reference to *The Wheels of Chance* appears on 4 December 1896 (*Diary*, p. 428).

5. Spiers and Coustillas, *Rediscovery*, p. 117.

6. Professor Coustillas has noted that Gissing drew some of these plot details from a notorious contemporary scandal publicized in the newspapers—the Druce-Portland affair. See Pierre Coustillas, "Introduction," *George Gissing: Essays & Fiction*, ed. Pierre Coustillas (Baltimore, 1970), p. 35n.

7. George Gissing, *The Town Traveller* (New York, 1898), ch. i, p. 6; hereafter referred to in the text by chapter and page number.

8. *Letters to Fleury*, 26 March 1899, p. 122.

9. *Diary*, 6, 10, and 15 July 1898, p. 497.

10. *Letters to Fleury*, 26 August 1898, p. 49.

11. George Gissing, *The Crown of Life* (New York, 1899), ch. viii, p. 62; hereafter referred to in the text by chapter and page number.

12. *Letters to Fleury*, late July to 5 August 1898, pp. 27–31.

13. On Britain's African empire and on Rhodes, see Ensor, *England 1870–1914*, pp. 189–94, 212–13, 225–29, 232–34.

14. Korg, *GG*, p. 236.

15. Dyce bases his theory on an actual work: Jean Izoulet, *La Cité moderne: métaphysique de la sociologie* [The Modern City: The Metaphysics of Sociology] (Paris: F. Alcan, 1894). Izoulet argues for a socialism governed by a naturally evolving aristocracy of talent.

16. Ensor, *England 1870–1914*, p. 444.

17. George Gissing, *Our Friend the Charlatan* (New York, 1901), ch. xviii, 234; hereafter referred to in the text by chapter and page number.

18. See Robert Blake, *Disraeli* (New York: St. Martin's Press, 1967), pp. 150–61, 769–71. For a detailed account of the courtship and marriage from the viewpoint of Disrael's wife, see Mollie Hardwick, *Mrs. Dizzy: The Life of Mary Anne Disraeli, Viscountess Beaconsfield* (New York: St. Martin's Press, 1972), pp. 37–136.

19. Spiers and Coustillas, *Rediscovery*, pp. 150–51. For another, briefer, account of the grocery business, see *The Unclassed*, ch. xxxv, pp. 282–87.

20. George Gissing, *Will Warburton: A Romance of Real Life* (London, 1905), ch. xlvi, p. 325; hereafter referred to in the text by chapter and page number.

21. For details about Britain's great agricultural depression, see Herman Ausubel, *The Late Victorians: A Short History* (New York: Nostrand, 1955), pp. 12–17, 97–100, 108–11.

22. Gissing began researching his Roman novel as far back as 1897. See Korg, *GG*, p. 211. For other Victorian novels about Rome's fall, see Doris B. Kelly, "A Check List of Nineteenth-Century Fiction about the Decline of Rome," *Bulletin of the New York Public Library* 72 (June 1968):400–13.

23. Spiers and Coustillas, *Rediscovery*, pp. 153–54.

24. For the hero's protracted illness, see George Gissing, *Veranilda:*

A Romance (London, 1904), ch. xxi, 243–46, 252–54; ch. xxiv, 275–81; hereafter referred to in the text by chapter and page number.

25. See *Diary*, 3 June 1897, p. 436: "Reading Gibbon on Justinian."

26. See above, "Preface."

Chapter Eight

1. Over the years, Gissing's seven miscellaneous short-story collections have remained largely out of print. Some are hard to find even in good libraries. Soon, however, Professor Coustillas's planned collection of Gissing's complete short stories may rescue them from undeserved neglect. The total of 110 remains tentative. For the most recent discovery of Gissing stories, see "Unknown Gissing Stories from Chicago," pp. 1417–18. For an indispensable, although provisional, bibliography of Gissing's short stories, see Pierre Coustillas, "Gissing's Short Stories: A Bibliography," *English Literature in Transition* 7, no. 2 (1964):59–72. Among the smattering of criticism on Gissing's short fiction, two essays deserve mention: J. M. Mitchell, "Notes on George Gissing's Short Stories," *Studies in English Literature* (Tokyo) 38 (March 1962):195–205; W. V. Harris, "An Approach to Gissing's Short Stories," *Studies in Short Fiction* 2 (Winter 1965):137–44. The finest short stories appear in George Gissing, *Human Odds and Ends: Stories and Sketches* (London, 1898), hereafter referred to in the text as *HOE*; George Gissing, *The House of Cobwebs*, with an Introduction by Thomas Seccombe (London 1931; first pub. 1906), hereafter referred to in the text as *HC*; George Gissing, *A Victim of Circumstances and Other Stories*, with a Preface by Alfred C. Gissing (Boston, 1927), hereafter referred to in the text as *VC*. A later collection seems inferior to the previous three: George Gissing, *Stories and Sketches* (London, 1938); hereafter referred to in the text as *SS*. Two other collections contain Gissing's immature stories written in the United States in 1877: George Gissing, *Sins of the Fathers and Other Tales*, with an Introduction by Vincent Starrett (Chicago, 1924); George Gissing, *Brownie*, with six other stories attributed to him, with Introduction by George Everett Hastings, Vincent Starrett, and Thomas Ollive Mabbott (New York, 1931). Previously unpublished stories are printed from the extant manuscripts in George Gissing, *Essays & Fiction* (Baltimore, 1970), ed., with an introduction, by Pierre Coustillas; hereafter referred to in the text as *EF*.

2. For the argument that Gissing's fiction (particularly *New Grub Street*) influenced James's tales about authors, see Adeline R. Tintner, "Some Notes for a Study of the Gissing Phase in Henry James's Fiction," *GN* 16 (July 1980):1–15.

3. On the Victorian fondness for historical paintings, see William Gaunt, *The Restless Century: Painting in Britain 1800–1900* (London: Phaidon, 1972), p. 20, as well as the many plates of this genre scattered throughout the volume.

4. *Dictionary of National Biography* (1917 ed.; rpt. 1921–22 and 1937–38), s.v. "Cox, David" and "Fielding, Anthony Vandyke Copley." See Gaunt, pl. 57, for a reproduction of Cox's *A Windy Day* (1850).

5. On this point and on other problems faced by Victorian female painters, see Linda Nochlin, "Why Are There No Great Women Artists?" in *Woman in Sexist Society: Studies in Power and Powerlessness*, ed. Vivian Gornick and Barbara K. Moran (New York: Mentor, 1972), pp. 480–510.

6. Simone de Beauvoir, *The Second Sex*, tr. H. M. Parshley (New York, Alfred A. Knopf, 1957), p. 684.

7. Ibid.

8. Ibid., p. 685.

9. Somewhat unusually for Gissing, these are obvious type names. In colloquial English, *don* means a head, fellow, or tutor of a college. *Argent* (silver) suggests wealth.

10. On the connection between women's bicycling and their shortened skirts after 1889, see Ensor, *England 1870–1914*, p. 338.

11. Houghton, *Victorian Frame of Mind*, p. 357.

12. Quoted from William Acton, *The Function and Disorders of the Reproductive Organs* [(London?], 1857), by Steven Marcus, *The Other Victorians: A Study of Sexuality and Pornography in Mid-Nineteenth-Century England* (New York: Bantam, 1967), p. 24.

13. *Diary*, 25 April 1888, p. 27.

14. George Moore, *Confessions of a Young Man: Edited and Annotated by George Moore 1904 and Again in 1916* (New York: Capricorn Books, 1959), ch. vi, pp. 57–58.

Chapter Nine

1. Edmund Wilson, *The Wound and the Bow* (Boston: Houghton

Mifflin, 1941), p. 2; Edward Garnett, "Fiction," *Speaker* 14 (26 May 1906):190–91; Cyril Connolly, "The Legacy of Gissing," *Sunday Times* (London), 25 January 1953, p. 5.

2. *Critical Studies of the Works of Charles Dickens* contains "*Sketches by Boz*," "*The Pickwick Papers*," "*Oliver Twist*," "*Nicholas Nickleby*," "*Martin Chuzzlewit*," "*Dombey and Son*," "*Barnaby Rudge*," "*The Old Curiosity Shop*," "*Bleak House*," plus "Dickens in Memory"—a personal reminiscence about Dickens's works, first published in *Literature*, 21 December 1901, pp. 572–75. See Pierre Coustillas, *Gissing's Writings on Dickens: A Bio-bibliographical Survey, Together with Two Uncollected Reviews by George Gissing from The Times Literary Supplement* (London, 1969), pp. 1–16. Perceptive analyses of Gissing's Dickens criticism appear in Goode, *GG*, pp. 13–40, and in Korg, *GG*, pp. 215–19.

3. George Gissing, *Critical Studies of the Works of Charles Dickens* (New York, 1965), p. 29; hereafter referred to in the text as *CS*, with chapter headings and page numbers.

4. René Wellek, "Literature and Society," in *Theory of Literature*, by René Wellek and Austin Warren (New York: Harcourt, Brace & World, 1956), p. 84.

5. George Gissing, *Charles Dickens: A Critical Study* (St. Clair Shores, Mich., 1976), ch. viii, p. 204; hereafter referred to in the text as *CD*, with chapter and page number. This edition reprints the 1904 New York edition. The first edition was that of London, 1898.

6. See above, "Preface."

7. Gissing's south Italian trip lasted from 16 November to 12 December 1897 (*Diary*, pp. 455–73).

8. Dean MacCannell, *The Tourist: A New Theory of the Leisure Class* (New York: Schocken Books, 1976), pp. 42–45.

9. George Gissing, *By the Ionian Sea: Notes of a Ramble in Southern Italy* (London, 1905), ch. iii, pp. 25–29; hereafter referred to in the text by chapter and page number. For Gissing's identification of his guidebooks as Murray and Baedeker, see *Diary*, 10 December 1897, p. 470.

10. The words come from Horace's sixth ode in his second book of *Odes*. For a verse translation, see *The Odes of Horace*, tr. James Michie, with the complete Latin text (New York: Washington Square Press, 1965), pp. 88–91.

11. *Diary*, 8 December 1897, p. 467.

12. MacCannell, *Tourist*, pp. 92–102.

13. A first draft of *Ryecroft* was written from 1 September to 23 October 1900. It was rewritten and expanded in August and September 1901; was serialized as "An Author at Grass," in the *Fortnightly Review* 325 (May 1902–February 1903); and in 1903 was ultimately published as *The Private Papers of Henry Ryecroft.*

14. On *Ryecroft*'s genre, see Pierre Coustillas, "Introduction and Notes," *Les Carnets d'Henry Ryecroft* [The Private Papers of Henry Ryecroft], by George Gissing, ed. and tr. Pierre Coustillas, bilingual ed. (Paris, 1966), pp. 9–73, 497–542. The usually perceptive Walter Allen seems unjust in calling the *Ryecroft* papers a "repellent" "autobiographical fantasia . . . , a dream of . . . irresponsibility." Allen's negative judgment appears all the more surprising in view of his praise for *The Odd Women*, which contains a far cruder fantasy of escape from work in the character of the globe-trotting Barfoot (*The English Novel*, pp. 343, 349).

15. George Gissing, "Autumn," *The Private Papers of Henry Ryecroft* (New York, 1927), p. 151; hereafter referred to in the text by chapter name and page number. Gissing's manuscript "Commonplace Book," held by the New York Public Library, has been published as *George Gissing's Commonplace Book*, ed. with introduction by Jacob Korg (New York, 1962). Gissing's manuscript "Memorandum Book," held by the Huntington Library, at present remains unpublished.

16. Just before Ryecroft's death, he is ten years older than his creator: Gissing was not quite forty-three when he finished the book's first draft ("Spring," *Ryecroft*, p. 24).

17. *The Odd Women*, ch. ix, p. 89; ch. xvii, p. 178.

Chapter Ten

1. Unsigned review, *World* (London), 29 April 1891, p. 28; reprinted in *Gissing: The Critical Heritage*, ed. Pierre Coustillas and Colin Partridge (London, 1972), p. 172. This volume contains a copious collection of reviews and articles on Gissing from 1880 to 1912. For a useful annotated secondary bibliography covering 1880–1970, see Joseph J. Wolff, ed., *George Gissing: An Annotated Bibliography of Writings about Him* (De Kalb, Ill., 1974).

2. Coustillas and Partridge, *Gissing: The Critical Heritage*, pp. 338–47.

3. Christopher Morley, "A Note on George Gissing," *Saturday Review of Literature* (New York) 3 (14 May 1927):821; Conrad Aiken, "George Gissing," *Dial* 83 (December 1927):512–14; Malcolm Cowley, "What the Revolutionary Movement Can Do for a Writer," *New Masses* 15 (7 May 1935):20–22; Malcolm Cowley, *Exile's Return* (New York: Viking, 1934), p. 20.

4. George Orwell, "George Gissing," in *Collected Articles on George Gissing*, ed. Pierre Coustillas (New York, 1968), pp. 54–55, 50, 51, 56, 52–54. This posthumously published Orwell essay first appeared in *London Magazine* 7 (June 1960):36–43.

5. Adrian Poole, *Gissing in Context* (Totowa, N.J., 1975).

6. John Goode, "George Gissing's *The Nether World*," in *Tradition and Tolerance in Nineteenth-Century Fiction*, pp. 207–41; John Goode, "Gissing, Morris and English Socialism," *Victorian Studies* 12 (December 1968):201–26; John Goode, *George Gissing: Ideology and Fiction*.

7. Robert L. Selig, " 'The Valley of the Shadow of Books': Alienation in Gissing's *New Grub Street*," *Nineteenth-Century Fiction* 25 (September 1970):188–98; John Gross, "Introduction," *New Grub Street* (London, 1967), pp. v-xii; Bernard Bergonzi, "The Novelist as Hero," *Twentieth Century* 164 (November 1958):444–55.

8. Maria Teresa Chialant, "*The Odd Women* di George Gissing, e il movimento femminista" [George Gissing's *The Odd Women* and the Feminist Movement], *Annali Istituto Universitario Orientale, Napoli, Sezione Germanica* 10 (1967):155–87; Nina Auerbach, *Communities of Women: An Idea in Fiction*, pp. 141–57.

9. See above, "Preface."

10. Orwell, "George Gissing," p. 51.

Selected Bibliography

PRIMARY SOURCES

When only one edition appears, this is the first edition. When multiple editions are listed, the first edition appears first. An asterisk following the publication date indicates an edition cited in the text.

1. Published Works

A. Novels

Born in Exile: A Novel. 3 vols. London: A. & C. Black, 1892. London: Thomas Nelson, [1913].*

The Crown of Life. London: Methuen, 1899. New York: Frederick A. Stokes, 1899.*

Demos: A Story of English Socialism. 3 vols. London: Smith, Elder, 1886. New York: E. P. Dutton, [1928].*

Denzil Quarrier: A Novel. London: Lawrence & Bullen, 1892. New York: Macmillan, 1892.*

The Emancipated: A Novel. 3 vols. London: Bentley, 1890. Chicago: Way & Williams, 1895.* Later edition based on 1893 Lawrence & Bullen first one-volume edition. Edited by Pierre Coustillas. Hassocks, Sussex: Harvester Press, 1977.

Eve's Ransom. London: Lawrence & Bullen, 1895. New York: D. Appleton, 1895.*

In the Year of Jubilee. 3 vols. London: Lawrence & Bullen, 1894.* Later edition based on 1895 Lawrence & Bullen edition. Edited by P. F. Kropholler. Introduction by Gillian Tindall. Hassocks, Sussex: Harvester Press, 1976.

Isabel Clarendon. 2 vols. London: Chapman & Hall, 1886. Later edition based on first edition. Edited by Pierre Coustillas. 2 vols. Brighton, Sussex: Harvester Press, 1969.*

A Life's Morning. 3 vols. London: Smith, Elder, 1888. New York: E. P. Dutton, [1914].*

The Nether World: A Novel. 3 vols. London: Smith, Elder, 1889. London: Dent, Everyman's Library, 1973; New York: Dutton, Everyman's Library, 1973.*

New Grub Street: A Novel. 3 vols. London: Smith, Elder, 1891. New York: Modern Library, 1926.* Harmondsworth, Middlesex: Penguin, 1968.

The Odd Women. 3 vols. London: Lawrence & Bullen, 1893. New York: W. W. Norton, 1971.* London: Virago, 1980.

Our Friend the Charlatan: A Novel. London: Chapman & Hall, 1901. New York: Henry Holt, 1901.* Later edition based on first English edition. Edited by Pierre Coustillas. Hassocks, Sussex: Harvester Press, 1976.

The Paying Guest. London: Cassell, 1895. New York: Dodd, Mead, 1895.*

Sleeping Fires. London: T. Fisher Unwin, 1895. New York: D. Appleton, 1896.*

Thyrza: A Tale. 3 vols. London: Smith, Elder, 1887. Revised edition. London: Smith, Elder, 1891. American edition based on revised Smith, Elder edition. New York: E. P. Dutton, [1928].*

The Town Traveller. London: Methuen, 1898. New York: Frederick A. Stokes, 1898.*

The Unclassed: A Novel. 3 vols. London: Chapman & Hall, 1884. Revised edition. London: Lawrence & Bullen, 1895. Later edition based on revised Lawrence & Bullen ed. London: A. H. Bullen, 1901.*

Veranilda: A Romance. London: Archibald Constable, 1904.*

The Whirlpool. London: Lawrence & Bullen, 1897. New York: Frederick A. Stokes, 1897.*

Will Warburton: A Romance of Real Life. London: Archibald Constable, 1905.*

Workers in the Dawn: A Novel. 3 vols. London: Remington, 1880. Later edition edited by Robert Shafer. 2 vols. Garden City, N.Y.: Doubleday, Doran, 1935.*

B. Literary Criticism, Travel Memoirs, Fictionalized Journals, Essays

By the Ionian Sea: Notes of a Ramble in Southern Italy. London: Chapman & Hall, 1901. London: Chapman & Hall, 1905.*

Charles Dickens: A Critical Study. London: Blackie, 1898. New York: Dodd, Mead, 1898. New York: Dodd, Mead, 1904. Reprint of 1904 Dodd, Mead edition. St. Clair Shores, Mich.: Scholarly Press, 1976.*

Critical Studies of the Works of Charles Dickens. New York: Greenberg, 1924. Reprint. New York: Haskell House, 1965.*

Essays & Fiction. Edited by Pierre Coustillas. Baltimore: Johns Hopkins Press, 1970.*

Notes on Social Democracy. Edited by Jacob Korg. London: Enitharmon Press, 1968.

The Private Papers of Henry Ryecroft. London: Constable, 1903. New York: E. P. Dutton, Everyman's Library, 1927.*

C. Short Stories

Brownie. New York: Columbia University Press, 1931.*

Essays & Fiction. Edited by Pierre Coustillas. Baltimore: Johns Hopkins Press, 1970.*

The House of Cobwebs and Other Stories. London: Constable, 1906. London: Constable, 1931.*

Human Odds and Ends. London: Lawrence & Bullen, 1898.*

Sins of the Fathers and Other Tales. Chicago: Pascal Covici, 1924.*

Stories and Sketches. London: Michael Joseph, 1938.*

"A Test of Honor." In "Unknown Gissing Stories from Chicago." By Pierre Coustillas and Robert L. Selig. *Times Literary Supplement* (London), 12 December 1980, pp. 1417–18.

A Victim of Circumstances and Other Stories. London: Constable, 1927. Boston: Houghton Mifflin, 1927.*

D. Letters, Diaries, Commonplace Books

George Gissing and H. G. Wells: Their Friendship and Correspondence. Edited by Royal A. Gettmann. Urbana: University of Illinois Press, 1961.*

George Gissing's Commonplace Book: A Manuscript in the Berg Collection of the New York Public Library. Edited by Jacob Korg. New York: New York Public Library, 1962.*

The Letters of George Gissing to Eduard Bertz, 1887–1903. Edited by

Arthur C. Young. New Brunswick, N.J.: Rutgers University Press, 1961.*

The Letters of George Gissing to Gabrielle Fleury. Edited by Pierre Coustillas. New York: The New York Public Library, Astor, Lenox and Tilden Foundations, 1964.*

Letters of George Gissing to Members of His Family. Collected and arranged by Algernon and Ellen Gissing. London: Constable, 1927.*

London and the Life of Literature in Late Victorian England: The Diary of George Gissing, Novelist. Edited by Pierre Coustillas. Lewisburg, Pa.: Bucknell University Press, 1978.*

E. Selected Writings

Selections Autobiographical and Imaginative from the Works of George Gissing. Edited by Alfred C. Gissing. London: Jonathan Cape, 1929.

2. Unpublished Materials

New Haven. Beinecke Rare Book and Manuscript Library, Yale University. Letters, notebooks, and miscellaneous documents of George Gissing.

New York. Henry W. and Albert A. Berg Collection of the New York Public Library, Astor, Lenox and Tilden Foundations. Letters of George Gissing.

SECONDARY SOURCES

1. Bibliographies

Collie, Michael. *George Gissing: A Bibliography*. Toronto: University of Toronto Press, 1975. As of 1981, the only existing comprehensive bibliography on Gissing's publications, but marred by many factual and typographical errors.

Coustillas, Pierre. "Gissing's Short Stories: A Bibliography." *English Literature in Transition* 7, no. 2 (1964):59–72. An indispensable, although provisional, bibliography. Since its publication, two previously unknown stories have been discovered.

Wolff, Joseph J., comp. and ed. *George Gissing: An Annotated*

Bibliography of Writings about Him. De Kalb: Northern Illinois University Press, 1974. A useful work, covering 1880 to 1970.

2. Books

Collie, Michael. *The Alien Art: A Critical Study of George Gissing's Novels*. Folkestone, Kent: William Dawson, 1979. Useful for its genetic textual criticism but unreliable in its straight literary criticism.

———. *George Gissing: A Biography*. Folkestone, Kent: William Dawson, 1977. Marred by factual errors and by speculations presented as facts.

Coustillas, Pierre. *Gissing's Writings on Dickens: A Bio-bibliographical Survey, Together with Two Uncollected Reviews by George Gissing from the Times Literary Supplement*. London: Enitharmon Press, 1969. An informative short account of Gissing's Dickens criticism.

———, and Partridge, Colin, eds. *Gissing: The Critical Heritage*. London: Routledge & Kegan Paul, 1972. Contains a copious collection of reviews and articles on Gissing from 1880 to 1912, supplemented by a full list of other pieces from this period.

Donnelly, Mabel Collins. *George Gissing: Grave Comedian*. Cambridge, Mass.: Harvard University Press, 1954. Flawed by critical unsophistication and by spotty research concerning Gissing's life, but often shows good taste in specifying the writer's best works.

Goode, John. *George Gissing: Ideology and Fiction*. New York: Barnes & Noble, 1979. Analyzes the ideological implications of Gissing's works within an economic and historical framework. Stimulating and intelligent but burdened with unnecessary Marxist jargon.

Gordan, John D. *George Gissing, 1857–1903: An Exhibition from the Berg Collection*. New York: New York Public Library, 1954. Useful short account of Gissing's life and publications.

Korg, Jacob. *George Gissing: A Critical Biography*. Seattle: University of Washington Press, 1963. Essential for students of Gissing because of its perceptive placing of the novelist's life and writings within the framework of late-Victorian culture.

Poole, Adrian. *Gissing in Context*. Totowa, N.J.: Rowman & Littlefield, 1975. An intelligent analysis of Gissing's literary qualities and a comparison of him with other major Victorian novelists, including Hardy, Meredith, Dickens, Thackeray, and Charlotte Brontë.

Roberts, Morley. *The Private Life of Henry Maitland*. London: Nash, 1912. The first published biography of Gissing. Marred by its semifictionalized form and its unsubstantiated gossip.

Spiers, John, and Coustillas, Pierre. *The Rediscovery of George Gissing: A Reader's Guide*. London: National Book League, 1971. An informative short survey of Gissing's life and work.

Swinnerton, Frank. *George Gissing: A Critical Study*. London: Martin Secker, 1912. A largely hostile analysis of Gissing's works—an analysis often colored by the critic's predilection for high-Victorian idealism.

Tindall, Gillian. *The Born Exile: George Gissing*. London: Temple Smith, 1974. Perceptive criticism about the relationship of Gissing's life to his work.

3. Parts of Books

Allen, Walter. *The English Novel: A Short Critical History*. New York: E. P. Dutton, 1958, pp. 339–50. A perceptive and largely appreciative discussion of Gissing's achievements as a novelist.

————. "Introduction." In *The Nether World*, by George Gissing. London: Dent, Everyman's Library, 1973; New York: Dutton, Everyman's Library, 1973, pp. v–xvii. Excellent analysis of the novel's power in depicting social misery.

Auerbach, Nina. *Communities of Women: An Idea in Fiction*. Cambridge, Mass.: Harvard University Press, 1978, pp. 141–57. A stimulating feminist analysis of *The Odd Women*. Praises Gissing's sympathetic depiction of an all-female community.

Coustillas, Pierre. "Introduction." In *George Gissing: Essays & Fiction*. Edited by Pierre Coustillas. Baltimore: Johns Hopkins, 1970, pp. 1–70. Contains much valuable miscellaneous information about Gissing and his works.

————. "Introduction." In *Isabel Clarendon*, by George Gissing. Brighton, Sussex: Harvester Press, 1969, 1:xv–lx. A detailed and helpful disussion of the novel's genesis, critical reception, and literary qualities.

————. "Introduction and Notes." In *Les Carnets d'Henry Ryecroft* [The Private Papers of Henry Ryecroft], by George Gissing.

Edited and translated into French by Pierre Coustillas. Bilingual ed. Paris: Aubrier-Montaigne, 1966, pp. 9–73, 494–542. Contains an illuminating critical and scholarly apparatus.

Gettmann, Royal A. *A Victorian Publisher: A Study of the Bentley Papers*. Cambridge: Cambridge University Press, 1960, pp. 215–22. An important account of Gissing's publishing misadventures with Bentley.

[Gissing, T. W.] "Margaret." In *Margaret and Other Poems by an East Anglian*. London: Simpkin, Marshall, 1855, pp. 1–23. A poem by Gissing's father that influenced the son's attitudes in his relationship with the prostitute Nell Harrison. Highly significant for an understanding of the novelist's life.

Goode, John. "George Gissing's *The Nether World*." In *Tradition and Tolerance in Nineteenth-Century Fiction: Critical Essays on Some English and American Novels*, by David Howard, John Lucas, and John Goode. London: Routledge & Kegan Paul, 1966, pp. 207–41. Perceptively discusses the book's treatment of povetry as an inescapable social force.

Gross, John. "Introduction." In *New Grub Street*, by George Gissing. London: Bodley Head, 1967, pp. v–xii. An important discussion of Gissing's novels. Praises *New Grub Street* as a portrait of writers' lives but warns against its melancholy personal bias.

Howe, Irving. "George Gissing: Poet of Fatigue." In his *A World More Attractive: A View of Modern Literature and Politics*. New York: Horizon Press, 1963, pp. 169–91. An excellent discussion of alienation both in Gissing's life and in *New Grub Street*.

Keating, P. J. *The Working Classes in Victorian Fiction*. London: Routledge & Kegan Paul, 1971. Helpful in placing Gissing among fellow Victorians who portrayed the working class in fiction: Dickens, Kingsley, Gaskell, Kipling, and others.

Korg, Jacob. "The Spiritual Theme of George Gissing's *Born in Exile*." In *From Jane Austen to Joseph Conrad: Essays Collected in Memory of James T. Hillhouse*. Edited by Robert C. Rathburn and Martin Steinmann. Minneapolis: University of Minnesota Press, 1958, pp. 246–56. An important comparison of Gissing's novel about spiritual alienation with similar novels by such Continental writers as Dostoevski, Turgenev, and Jacobsen.

Murry, J. Middleton. "George Gissing." In his *Katherine Mansfield and Other Literary Studies*. London: Constable, 1959, pp. 3–68.

Includes some perceptive remarks on Gissing's skillful portrayal of women.

Orwell, George. "George Gissing." In *Collected Articles on George Gissing*. Edited by Pierre Coustillas. New York: Barnes & Noble, 1968, pp. 50–57. A salute to a master of the shabby-genteel by a twentieth-century writer who owed much to Gissing. Insightful about Gissing's strengths.

Roberts, Morley. "Introduction." In *A Life's Morning*, by George Gissing. New York: E. P. Dutton, [1914], pp. v–ix. Includes an informative discussion of editorial changes in the book required by James Payn, the publisher's reader.

Wells, H. G. *Experiment in Autobiography*. London: V. Gollancz and the Cresset Press, 1934, 2:563, 567–81, 634. Provides somewhat condescending reminiscences about Gissing.

———. "The Novels of Mr. George Gissing." In *George Gissing and H. G. Wells: Their Friendship and Correspondence*. Edited by Royal A. Gettmann. Urbana: University of Illinois Press, 1961, pp. 242–59. Contains perceptive criticism about Gissing's use of "exponent" male characters.

4. Articles

Aiken, Conrad. "George Gissing." *Dial* 83 (December 1927):512–14. Significant praise of Gissing's short stories for their sad modernity.

Bergonzi, Bernard. "The Novelist as Hero." *Twentieth Century* 164 (November 1958):444–55. A valuable analysis of *New Grub Street*. Concludes that Gissing exaggerated the plight of authors.

Chialant, Maria Teresa. "*The Odd Women* di George Gissing, e il movimento femminista" [George Gissing's *The Odd Women* and the Feminist Movement]. *Annali Istituto Universitario Orientale, Napoli, Sezione Germanica* 10 (1967):155–87. An important analysis of the class-bound limitations in this novel's treatment of feminism.

Connolly, Cyril. "The Legacy of Gissing." *Sunday Times* (London), 25 January 1953, p. 5. Judiciously praises *The Private Papers of Henry Ryecroft* for "imaginative intensity."

Coustillas, P[ierre]. "George Gissing à Alderley Edge." *Études Anglaises* 20 (April-June 1967):174–78. Includes Gissing's essay "The Old School"—a revealing reminiscence about the Lindow Grove School.

———. "George Gissing à Manchester." *Études Anglaises* 16 (July-September 1963):255–61. Contains key documents about Gissing's college thefts, arrest, conviction, and imprisonment.

———. "Henry Hick's Recollections of George Gissing." *Huntington Library Quarterly* 29 (February 1966): 161–70. Valuable reminiscences by a close friend of Gissing's.

———, and Selig, Robert L. "Unknown Gissing Stories from Chicago." *Times Literary Supplement* (London), 12 December 1980, pp. 1417–18. Tells of recent discovery of Gissing's "A Mother's Hope" and "A Test of Honor." Gives plot summary of the first short story and the full text of the second.

Evans, Joyce. "Some Notes on *The Odd Women* and the Woman's Movement." *Gissing Newsletter* 2 (September 1966):1–4. Contains useful information about the Society for Promoting the Employment of Women—the model for the feminist school in the novel.

Garnett, Edward. "Fiction." *Speaker* 14 (26 May 1906):190–91. Contains a significant ranking of *By the Ionian Sea* as Gissing's finest work.

Goode, John. "Gissing, Morris and English Socialism." *Victorian Studies* 12 (December 1968):201–26. An important essay. Argues that *Demos* reflects late-Victorian fears of socialism rather than depicting actual Socialist ideology.

———, and Lelchuk, Alan. "Gissing's *Demos*: A Controversy." *Victorian Studies* 12 (June 1969):431–40. Goode argues for the relevance of cultural history in criticizing Gissing's novel, and Lelchuk argues for its fictional autonomy.

Harris, W. V. "An Approach to Gissing's Short Stories." *Studies in Short Fiction* 2 (Winter 1965):137–44. Makes an intelligent case for the impressiveness of Gissing's short fiction once he abandoned melodramatic plots and concentrated on humble characters faced with grubby problems.

Leavis, Q. D. "Gissing and the English Novel." *Scrutiny* 7 (June 1938):73–81. Important for ranking *New Grub Street* among the finest novels of nineteenth-century England.

Lelchuk, Alan. "*Demos*: The Ordeal of the Two Gissings." *Victorian Studies* 12 (March 1969):357–74. A stimulating but not wholly convincing commendation of *Demos*. Argues that its working-class vitality outweighs its anti-Socialist bias.

Mitchell, J. M. "Notes on George Gissing's Short Stories." *Studies in English Literature* (Tokyo) 38 (March 1962):195–205. A significantly favorable evaluation of Gissing's short fiction.

Roberts, Morley. "The Letters of George Gissing." *Virginia Quarterly Review* 7 (July 1931):409–26. Discusses Gissing's letters to Roberts and quotes extensively from one.

Selig, Robert L. "The Gospel of Work in *The Odd Women*: Gissing's Double Standard." *Supplement* to *Gissing Newsletter* 15 (January 1979):17–25. Finds a thematic incongruity in the novel: the feminist women proclaim the nobility of work, but the men detest all labor.

———. "A Sad Heart at the Late-Victorian Culture Market: George Gissing's *In the Year of Jubilee*." *Studies in English Literature* 9 (Autumn 1969):703–20. Provides detailed analysis of the novel's treatment of mass education, advertising, and popular songs.

———. " 'The Valley of the Shadow of Books': Alienation in Gissing's *New Grub Street*." *Nineteenth-Century Fiction* 25 (September 1970):188–98. Analyzes the novel's treatment of the alienating effects of both print and money.

Sichel, Edith. "Two Philanthropic Novelists: Mr. Walter Besant and Mr. George Gissing." *Murray's Magazine* 3 (April 1888):506–18. A characteristic late-Victorian reaction to the pessimism of Gissing's working-class novels.

Index

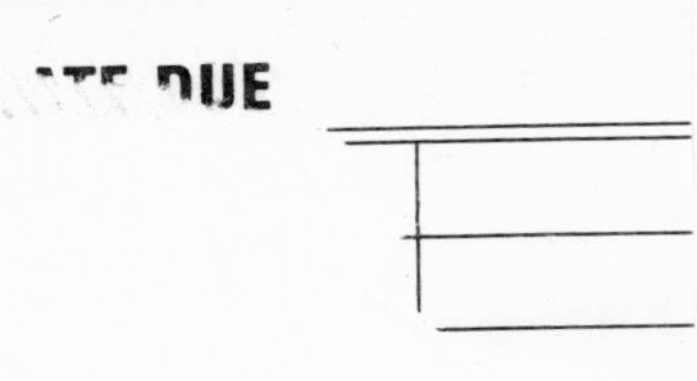
DUE